T0145607

Around the World in Seventy-Two Days

Around the World in Seventy-Two Days

Nellie Bly

MINT EDITIONS

Around the World in Seventy-Two Days was first published in 1890.

This edition published by Mint Editions 2021.

ISBN 9781513280066 | E-ISBN 9781513285085

Published by Mint Editions®

 MINT
EDITIONS

minteditionbooks.com

Publishing Director: Jennifer Newens
Design & Production: Rachel Lopez Metzger
Project Manager: Micaela Clark
Typesetting: Westchester Publishing Services

Contents

I

A Proposal to Girdle the Earth

What gave me the idea?

It is sometimes difficult to tell exactly what gives birth to an idea. Ideas are the chief stock in trade of newspaper writers and generally they are the scarcest stock in market, but they do come occasionally,

This idea came to me one Sunday. I had spent a greater part of the day and half the night vainly trying to fasten on some idea for a newspaper article. It was my custom to think up ideas on Sunday and lay them before my editor for his approval or disapproval on Monday. But ideas did not come that day and three o'clock in the morning found me weary and with an aching head tossing about in my bed. At last tired and provoked at my slowness in finding a subject, something for the week's work, I thought fretfully:

"I wish I was at the other end of the earth!"

"And why not?" the thought came: "I need a vacation; why not take a trip around the world?"

It is easy to see how one thought followed another. The idea of a trip around the world pleased me and I added: "If I could do it as quickly as Phileas Fogg did, I should go."

Then I wondered if it were possible to do the trip eighty days and afterwards I went easily off to sleep with the determination to know before I saw my bed again if Phileas Fogg's record could be broken.

I went to a steamship company's office that day and made a selection of time tables. Anxiously I sat down and went over them and if I had found the elixir of life I should not have felt better than I did when I conceived a hope that a tour of the world might be made in even less than eighty days.

I approached my editor rather timidly on the subject. I was afraid that he would think the idea too wild and visionary.

"Have you any ideas?" he asked, as I sat down by his desk.

"One," I answered quietly.

He sat toying with his pens, waiting for me to continue, so I blurted out:

"I want to go around the world!"

"Well?" he said, inquiringly looking up with a faint smile in his kind eyes.

"I want to go around in eighty days or less. I think I can beat Phileas Fogg's record. May I try it?"

To my dismay he told me that in the office they had thought of this same idea before and the intention was to send a man. However he offered me the consolation that he would favor my going, and then we went to talk with the business manager about it.

"It is impossible for you to do it," was the terrible verdict. "In the first place you are a woman and would need a protector, and even if it were possible for you to travel alone you would need to carry so much baggage that it would detain you in making rapid changes. Besides you speak nothing but English, so there is no use talking about it; no one but a man can do this."

"Very well," I said angrily, "Start the man, and I'll start the same day for some other newspaper and beat him."

"I believe you would," he said slowly. I would not say that this had any influence on their decision, but I do know that before we parted I was made happy by the promise that if any one was commissioned to make the trip, I should be that one.

After I had made my arrangements to go, other important projects for gathering news came up, and this rather visionary idea was put aside for a while.

One cold, wet evening, a year after this discussion, I received a little note asking me to come to the office at once. A summons, late in the afternoon, was such an unusual thing to me that I was to be excused if I spent all my time on the way to the office wondering what I was to be scolded for.

I went in and sat down beside the editor waiting for him to speak. He looked up from the paper on which he was writing and asked quietly: "Can you start around the world day after tomorrow?"

"I can start this minute," I answered, quickly trying to stop the rapid beating of my heart.

"We did think of starting you on the City of Paris tomorrow morning, so as to give you ample time to catch the mail train out of London. There is a chance if the Augusta Victoria, which sails the morning afterwards, has rough weather of your failing to connect with the mail train."

"I will take my chances on the Augusta Victoria, and save one extra day," I said.

The next morning I went to Ghormley, the fashionable dressmaker, to order a dress. It was after eleven o'clock when I got there and it took but very few moments to tell him what I wanted.

I always have a comfortable feeling that nothing is impossible if one applies a certain amount of energy in the right direction. When I want things done, which is always at the last moment, and I am met with such an answer: "It's too late. I hardly think it can be done;" I simply say:

"Nonsense! If you want to do it, you can do it. The question is, do you want to do it?"

I have never met the man or woman yet who was not aroused by that answer into doing their very best.

If we want good work from others or wish to accomplish anything ourselves, it will never do to harbor a doubt as to the result of an enterprise.

So, when I went to Ghormley's, I said to him: "I want a dress by this evening."

"Very well," he answered as unconcernedly as if it were an everyday thing for a young woman to order a gown on a few hours' notice.

"I want a dress that will stand constant wear for three months," I added, and then let the responsibility rest on him.

Bringing out several different materials he threw them in artistic folds over a small table, studying the effect in a pier glass before which he stood.

He did not become nervous or hurried. All the time that he was trying the different effects of the materials, he kept up a lively and half humorous conversation. In a few moments he had selected a plain blue broadcloth and a quiet plaid camel's-hair as the most durable and suitable combination for a traveling gown.

Before I left, probably one o'clock, I had my first fitting. When I returned at five o'clock for a second fitting, the dress was finished. I considered this promptness and speed a good omen and quite in keeping with the project.

After leaving Ghormley's I went to a shop and ordered an ulster. Then going to another dressmaker's, I ordered a lighter dress to carry with me to be worn in the land where I would find summer.

I bought one hand-bag with the determination to confine my baggage to its limit.

That night there was nothing to do but write to my few friends a line of farewell and to pack the hand-bag.

Packing that bag was the most difficult undertaking of my life; there was so much to go into such little space.

I got everything in at last except the extra dress. Then the question resolved itself into this: I must either add a parcel to my baggage or go around the world in and with one dress. I always hated parcels so I sacrificed the dress, but I brought out a last summer's silk bodice and after considerable squeezing managed to crush it into the hand-bag.

I think that I went away one of the most superstitious of girls. My editor had told me the day before the trip had been decided upon of an inauspicious dream he had had. It seemed that I came to him and told him I was going to run a race. Doubting my ability as a runner, he thought he turned his back so that he should not witness the race. He heard the band play, as it does on such occasions, and heard the applause that greeted the finish. Then I came to him with my eyes filled with tears and said: "I have lost the race."

"I can translate that dream," I said, when he finished; "I will start to secure some news and some one else will beat me."

When I was told the next day that I was to go around the world I felt a prophetic awe steal over me. I feared that Time would win the race and that I should not make the tour in eighty days or less.

Nor was my health good when I was told to go around the world in the shortest time possible at that season of the year. For almost a year I had been a daily sufferer from headache, and only the week previous I had consulted a number of eminent physicians fearing that my health was becoming impaired by too constant application to work. I had been doing newspaper work for almost three years, during which time I had not enjoyed one day's vacation. It is not surprising then that I looked on this trip as a most delightful and much needed rest.

The evening before I started I went to the office and was given £200 in English gold and Bank of England notes. The gold I carried in my pocket. The Bank of England notes were placed in a chamois-skin bag which I tied around my neck. Besides this I took some American gold and paper money to use at different ports as a test to see if American money was known outside of America.

Down in the bottom of my hand-bag was a special passport, number 247, signed by James G. Blaine, Secretary of State. Someone suggested that a revolver would be a good companion piece for the passport, but I had such a strong belief in the world's greeting me as I greeted it, that I refused to arm myself. I knew if my conduct was proper I should always find men ready to protect me, let them be Americans, English, French, German or anything else.

It is quite possible to buy tickets in New York for the entire trip, but I thought that I might be compelled to change my route at almost any point, so the only transportation I had provided on leaving New York was my ticket to London.

When I went to the office to say good-bye, I found that no itinerary had been made of my contemplated trip and there was some doubt as to whether the mail train which I expected to take to Brindisi, left London every Friday night. Nor did we know whether the week of my expected arrival in London was the one in which it connected with the ship for India or the ship for China. In fact when I arrived at Brindisi and found the ship was bound for Australia, I was the most surprised girl in the world.

I followed a man who had been sent to a steamship company's office to try to make out a schedule and help them arrange one as best they could on this side of the water. How near it came to being correct can be seen later on.

I have been asked very often since my return how many changes of clothing I took in my solitary hand-bag. Some have thought I took but one; others think I carried silk which occupies but little space, and others have asked if I did not buy what I needed at the different ports.

One never knows the capacity of an ordinary hand-satchel until dire necessity compels the exercise of all one's ingenuity to reduce every thing to the smallest possible compass. In mine I was able to pack two traveling caps, three veils, a pair of slippers, a complete outfit of toilet articles, ink-stand, pens, pencils, and copy-paper, pins, needles and thread, a dressing gown, a tennis blazer, a small flask and a drinking cup, several complete changes of underwear, a liberal supply of handkerchiefs and fresh ruchings and most bulky and uncompromising of all, a jar of cold cream to keep my face from chapping in the varied climates I should encounter.

That jar of cold cream was the bane of my existence. It seemed to take up more room than everything else in the bag and was always getting into just the place that would keep me from closing the satchel. Over my arm I carried a silk waterproof, the only provision I made against rainy weather. After-experience showed me that I had taken too much rather than too little baggage. At every port where I stopped at I could have bought anything from a ready-made dress down, except possibly at Aden, and as I did not visit the shops there I cannot speak from knowledge.

The possibilities of having any laundry work done during my rapid progress was one which had troubled me a good deal before starting. I had equipped myself on the theory that only once or twice in my journey would I be able to secure the services of a laundress. I knew that on the railways it would be impossible, but the longest railroad travel was the two days spent between London and Brindisi, and the four days between San Francisco and New York. On the Atlantic steamers they do no washing. On the Peninsular and Oriental steamers—which everyone calls the P. & O. boats—between Brindisi and China, the quartermaster turns out each day a wash that would astonish the largest laundry in America. Even if no laundry work was done on the ships, there are at all of the ports where they stop plenty of experts waiting to show what Orientals can do in the washing line. Six hours is ample time for them to perform their labors and when they make a promise to have work done in a certain time, they are prompt to the minute. Probably it is because they have no use for clothes themselves, but appreciate at its full value the money they are to receive for their labor. Their charges, compared with laundry prices in New York, are wonderfully low.

So much for my preparations. It will be seen that if one is traveling simply for the sake of traveling and not for the purpose of impressing one's fellow passengers, the problem of baggage becomes a very simple one. On one occasion—in Hong Kong, where I was asked to an official dinner—I regretted not having an evening dress with me, but the loss of that dinner was a very small matter when compared with the responsibilities and worries I escaped by not having a lot of trunks and boxes to look after.

II

The Start

On Thursday, November 14, 1889, at 9.40.30 o'clock, I started on my tour around the world.

Those who think that night is the best part of the day and that morning was made for sleep, know how uncomfortable they feel when for some reason they have to get up with—well, with the milkman.

I turned over several times before I decided to quit my bed. I wondered sleepily why a bed feels so much more luxurious, and a stolen nap that threatens the loss of a train is so much more sweet, than those hours of sleep that are free from duty's call. I half promised myself that on my return I would pretend sometime that it was urgent that I should get up so I could taste the pleasure of a stolen nap without actually losing anything by it. I dozed off very sweetly over these thoughts to wake with a start, wondering anxiously if there was still time to catch the ship.

Of course I wanted to go, but I thought lazily that if some of these good people who spend so much time in trying to invent flying machines would only devote a little of the same energy towards promoting a system by which boats and trains would always make their start at noon or afterwards, they would be of greater assistance to suffering humanity.

I endeavored to take some breakfast, but the hour was too early to make food endurable. The last moment at home came. There was a hasty kiss for the dear ones, and a blind rush downstairs trying to overcome the hard lump in my throat that threatened to make me regret the journey that lay before me.

"Don't worry," I said encouragingly, as I was unable to speak that dreadful word, goodbye; "only think of me as having a vacation and the most enjoyable time in my life."

Then to encourage myself I thought, as I was on my way to the ship: "It's only a matter of 28,000 miles, and seventy-five days and four hours, until I shall be back again."

A few friends who told of my hurried departure, were there to say good-bye. The morning was bright and beautiful, and everything seemed very pleasant while the boat was still; but when they were warned to go ashore, I began to realize what it meant for me.

"Keep up your courage," they said to me while they gave my hand the farewell clasp. I saw the moisture in their eyes and I tried to smile so that their last recollection of me would be one that would cheer them.

But when the whistle blew and they were on the pier, and I was on the Augusta Victoria, which was slowly but surely moving away from all I knew, taking me to strange lands and strange people, I felt lost. My head felt dizzy and my heart felt as if it would burst. Only seventy-five days! Yes, but it seemed an age and the world lost its roundness and seemed a long distance with no end, and—well, I never turn back.

I looked as long as I could at the people on the pier. I did not feel as happy as I have at other times in life. I had a sentimental longing to take farewell of everything.

"I am off," I thought sadly, "and shall I ever get back?"

Intense heat, bitter cold, terrible storms, shipwrecks, fevers, all such agreeable topics had been drummed into me until I felt much as I imagine one would feel if shut in a cave of midnight darkness and told that all sorts of horrors were waiting to gobble one up.

The morning was beautiful and the bay never looked lovelier. The ship glided out smoothly and quietly, and the people on deck looked for their chairs and rugs and got into comfortable positions, as if determined to enjoy themselves while they could, for they did not know what moment someone would be enjoying themselves at their expense.

When the pilot went off everybody rushed to the side of the ship to see him go down the little rope ladder. I watched him closely, but he climbed down and into the row boat, that was waiting to carry him to the pilot boat, without giving one glance back to us. It was an old story to him, but I could not help wondering if the ship should go down, whether there would not be some word or glance he would wish he had given.

"You have now started on your trip," someone said to me. "As soon as the pilot goes off and the captain assumes command, then, and only then our voyage begins, so now you are really started on your tour around the world."

Something in his words turned my thoughts to that demon of the sea—sea-sickness.

Never having taken a sea voyage before, I could expect nothing else than a lively tussle with the disease of the wave.

"Do you get sea-sick ?" I was asked in an interested, friendly way. That was enough; I flew to the railing.

Sick? I looked blindly down, caring little what the wild waves were saying, and gave vent to my feelings.

People are always unfeeling about sea-sickness. When I wiped the tears from my eyes and turned around, I saw smiles on the face of every passenger. I have noticed that they are always on the same side of the ship when one is taken suddenly, overcome, as it were, with one's own emotions.

The smiles did not bother me, but one man said sneeringly:

"And she's going around the world!"

I too joined in the laugh that followed. Silently I marveled at my boldness to attempt such a feat wholly unused, as I was, to sea-voyages. Still I did not entertain one doubt as to the result.

Of course I went to luncheon. Everybody did, and almost everybody left very hurriedly. I joined them, or, I don't know, probably I made the start. Anyway I never saw as many in the dining room at any one time during the rest of the voyage.

When dinner was served I went in very bravely and took my place on the Captain's left. I had a very strong determination to resist my impulses, but yet, in the bottom of my heart was a little faint feeling that I had found something even stronger than my will power.

Dinner began very pleasantly. The waiters moved about noiselessly, the band played an overture, Captain Albers, handsome and genial, took his place at the head, and the passengers who were seated at his table began dinner with a relish equaled only by enthusiastic wheelmen when roads are fine. I was the only one at the Captain's table who might be called an amateur sailor. I was bitterly conscious of this fact. So were the others.

I might as well confess it, while soup was being served, I was lost in painful thoughts and filled with a sickening fear. I felt that everything was just as pleasant as an unexpected gift on Christmas, and I endeavored to listen to the enthusiastic remarks about the music made by my companions, but my thoughts were on a topic that would not bear discussion.

I felt cold, I felt warm; I felt that I should not get hungry if I did not see food for seven days; in fact, I had a great, longing desire not to see it, nor to smell it, nor to eat of it, until I could reach land or a better understanding with myself.

Fish was served, and Captain Albers was in the midst of a good story when I felt I had more than I could endure.

"Excuse me," I whispered faintly, and then rushed, madly, blindly out. I was assisted to a secluded spot where a little reflection and a little unbridling of pent up emotion restored me to such a courageous state that I determined to take the Captain's advice and return to my unfinished dinner.

"The only way to conquer sea-sickness is by forcing one's self to eat," the Captain said, and I thought the remedy harmless enough to test.

They congratulated me on my return. I had a shamed feeling that I was going to misbehave again, but I tried to hide the fact from them. It came soon, and I disappeared at the same rate of speed as before.

Once again I returned. This time my nerves felt a little unsteady and my belief in my determination was weakening, Hardly had I seated myself when I caught an amused gleam of a steward's eye, which made me bury my face in my handkerchief and choke before I reached the limits of the dining hall.

The bravos with which they kindly greeted my third return to the table almost threatened to make me lose my bearings again. I was glad to know that dinner was just finished and I had the boldness to say that it was very good!

I went to bed shortly afterwards. No one had made any friends yet, so I concluded sleep would be more enjoyable than sitting in the music hall looking at other passengers engaged in the same first-day-at-sea occupation.

I went to bed shortly after seven o'clock. I had a dim recollection afterwards of waking up enough to drink some tea, but beyond this and the remembrance of some dreadful dreams, I knew nothing until I heard an honest, jolly voice at the door calling to me.

Opening my eyes I found the stewardess and a lady passenger in my cabin and saw the Captain standing at the door.

"We were afraid that you were dead," the Captain said when he saw that I was awake.

"I always sleep late in the morning," I said apologetically.

"In the morning!" the Captain exclaimed, with a laugh, which was echoed by the others, "It is half-past four in the evening!"

"But never mind," he added consolingly, "as long as you slept well it will do you good. Now get up and see if you can't eat a big dinner."

I did. I went through every course at dinner without flinching, and stranger still, I slept that night as well as people are commonly supposed to sleep after long exercise in the open air.

The weather was very bad, and the sea was rough, but I enjoyed it. My sea-sickness had disappeared, but I had a morbid, haunting idea,

NELLIE BLY

that although it was gone, it would come again, still I managed to make myself comfortable.

Almost all of the passengers avoided the dining-room, took their meals on deck and maintained reclining positions with a persistency that grew monotonous. One bright, clever, American-born girl was traveling alone to Germany, to her parents. She entered heartily into anything that was conducive to pleasure. She was a girl who talked a great deal and she always said something. I have rarely, if ever, met her equal. In German as well as English, she could ably discuss anything from fashions to politics. Her father and her uncle are men well-known in public affairs, and by this girl's conversation it was easy to see that she was a father's favorite child; she was so broad and brilliant and womanly. There was not one man on board who knew more about politics, art, literature or music, than this girl with Marguerite hair, and yet there was not one of us more ready and willing to take a race on deck than was she.

I think it is only natural for travelers to take an innocent pleasure in studying the peculiarities of their fellow companions. We were not out many days until everybody that was able to be about had added a little to their knowledge of those that were not. I will not say that the knowledge acquired in that way is of any benefit, nor would I try to say that those passengers who mingled together did not find one another as interesting and as fit subjects for comment. Nevertheless it was harmless and it afforded us some amusement.

I remember when I was told that we had among the passengers one man who counted his pulse after every meal, and they were hearty meals, too, for he was free from the disease of the wave, that I waited quite eagerly to have him pointed out, so that I might watch him. If it had been my pulse, instead of his own, that he watched so carefully, I could not have been more interested thereafter. Every day I became more anxious and concerned until I could hardly refrain from asking him if his pulse decreased before meals and increased afterwards, or if it was the same in the evening as it was in the morning.

I almost forgot my interest in this one man, when my attention was called to another, who counted the number of steps he took every day. This one in turn became less interesting when I found that one of the women, who had been a great sufferer from sea-sickness, had not undressed since she left her home in New York.

"I am sure we are all going down," she said one day in a burst of confidence, "and I am determined to go down dressed!"

I was not surprised after this that she was so dreadfully sea-sick.

One family who were removing from New York to Paris, had with them a little silver skye terrier, which bore the rather odd name of "Home, Sweet Home." Fortunately for the dog, as well as for those who were compelled to speak to him, they had shortened the name into "Homie."

"Homie's" passage was paid, but according to the rules of the ship, "Homie" was confined to the care of the butcher, much to the disgust of his master and mistress. "Homie" had not been accustomed to such harsh measures before, and the only streaks of happiness that came into his life were when permission was obtained for him to come on deck. Permission was granted with a proviso that if "Homie" barked he was to be taken instantly below. I fear that many hours of "Homie's" imprisonment might be laid at our door, for he knew how to dig most frantically when anyone said, "Rats," and when he did dig, he usually punctuated his attempt with short, crisp barks. With dismay we daily noted "Homie's" decrease in flesh. We marveled at his losing weight while confined in the butcher's quarters, and at last put it down to sea-sickness, which he, like some of the passengers, confined to the secrecy of his cabin. Towards the end of the voyage, when we were all served with sausage and Hamburger steak, there would be many whispered inquiries as to whether "Homie" had been seen that day. So anxious became those whispers that sometimes I thought they were rather tinged with a personal concern that was not wholly friendship for the wee dog.

When everything else grew tiresome, Captain Albers would always invent something to amuse us. He made a practice every evening after dinner, of putting the same number of lines on a card as there were gentlemen at the table. One of these lines he would mark and then partly folding the card over so as to prevent the marked line from being seen. would pass it around for the men to take their choice.

After all had marked, the card was passed to the Captain, and we would wait breathlessly for the verdict. The gentleman whose name had been marked paid for the cigars or cordials for the others.

Many were the discussions about the erroneous impression entertained by most foreigners about Americans and America. Some one remarked that the majority of people in foreign lands were not able to tell where the United States is.

"There are plenty of people who think the United States is one little island, with a few houses on it," Captain Albers said. "Once there was delivered at my house, near the wharf, in Hoboken, a letter from Germany, addressed to,

> 'CAPTAIN ALBERS,
> FIRST HOUSE IN AMERICA.'"

"I got one from Germany once," said the most bashful man at the table, his face flushing at the sound of his own voice, "addressed to,

> 'HOBOKEN, OPPOSITE THE UNITED STATES.'"

While at luncheon on the 21st of November, some one called out that we were in sight of land. The way everyone left the table and rushed on deck was surely not surpassed by the companions of Columbus when they discovered America. I can not give any good reason for it, but I know that I looked at the first point of bleak land with more interest than I would have bestowed on the most beautiful bit of scenery in the world.

We had not been long in sight of land until the decks began to fill with dazed-looking, wan-faced people. It was just as if we had taken on new passengers. We could not realize that they were from New York and had been enjoying a season of seclusion since leaving that port.

Dinner that evening was a very pleasant affair. Extra courses had been prepared in honor of those that were leaving at Southampton. I had not known one of the passengers when I left New York seven days before, but I realized, now that I was so soon to separate from them, that I regretted the parting very much.

Had I been traveling with a companion I should not have felt this so keenly, for naturally then I would have had less time to cultivate the acquaintance of my fellow passengers.

They were all so kind to me that I should have been the most ungrateful of women had I not felt that I was leaving friends behind. Captain Albers had served many years as commander of a ship in Eastern seas, and he cautioned me as to the manner in which I should take care of my health. As the time grew shorter for my stay on the Augusta Victoria, some teased me gently as to the outcome of my attempt to beat the record made by a hero of fiction, and I found myself forcing a false gaiety that helped to hide my real fears.

The passengers on the Augusta Victoria all stayed up to see us off. We sat on deck talking or nervously walking about until half-past two in the morning. Then some one said the tugboat had come alongside, and we all rushed over to see it. After it was made secure we went down to the lower deck to see who would come on and to get some news from land.

One man was very much concerned about my making the trip to London alone. He thought as it was so late, or rather so early, that the London correspondent, who was to have met me, would not put in an appearance.

"I shall most certainly leave the ship here and see you safely to London, if no one comes to meet you," he protested, despite my assurances that I felt perfectly able to get along safely without an escort.

More for his sake than my own, I watched the men come on board, and tried to pick out the one that had been sent to meet me. Several of them were passing us in a line just as a gentleman made some remark about my trip around the world. A tall young man overheard the remark, and turning at the foot of the stairs, looked down at me with a hesitating smile.

"Nellie Bly?" he asked inquiringly.

"Yes," I replied, holding out my hand, which he gave a cordial grasp, meanwhile asking if I had enjoyed my trip, and if my baggage was ready to be transferred.

The man who had been so fearful of my traveling to London alone, took occasion to draw the correspondent into conversation. Afterwards he came to me and said with the most satisfied look upon his face:

"He is all right. If he had not been so, I should have gone to London with you anyway. I can rest satisfied now for he will take care of you."

I went away with a warm feeling in my heart for that kindly man who would have sacrificed his own comfort to insure the safety of an unprotected girl.

A few warm hand clasps, and interchanging of good wishes, a little dry feeling in the throat, a little strained pulsation of the heart, a little hurried run down the perpendicular plank to the other passengers who were going to London, and then the tug cast off from the ship, and we drifted away in the dark.

III

Southampton to Jules Verne's

"M r. & Mrs. Jules Verne have sent a special letter asking that if possible you will stop to see them," the London correspondent said to me, as we were on our way to the wharf.

"Oh, how I should like to see them!" I exclaimed, adding in the same breath, "Isn't it hard to be forced to decline such a treat?"

"If you are willing to go without sleep and rest for two nights, I think it can be done," he said quietly.

"Safely? Without making me miss any connections? If so, don't think about sleep or rest."

"It depends on our getting a train out of here to-night. All the regular trains until morning have left, and unless they decide to run a special mail train for the delayed mails, we will have to stay here all night and that will not give us time to see Verne. We shall see when we land what they will decide to do."

The boat that was landing us left much to be desired in the way of comfort. The only cabin seemed to be the hull, but it was filled with mail and baggage and lighted by a lamp with a smoked globe. I did not see any place to sit down, so we all stood on deck, shivering in the damp, chilly air, and looking in the gray fog like uneasy spirits.

The dreary, dilapidated wharf was a fit landing place for the antique boat. I silently followed the correspondent into a large empty shed, where a few men with sleep in their eyes and uniforms that bore ample testimony to the fact that they had slept in their clothes, were stationed behind some long, low tables.

"Where are your keys?" the correspondent asked me as he sat my solitary bag down before one of these weary looking inspectors.

"It is too full to lock," I answered simply.

"Will you swear that you have no tobacco or tea?" the inspector asked my escort lazily.

"Don't swear," I said to him; then turning to the inspector I added: "It's my bag."

He smiled and putting a chalk mark upon the bag freed us.

"Declare your tobacco and tea or tip the man," I said teazingly to a passenger who stood with poor, thin, shaking "Homie" under one arm, searching frantically through his pockets for his keys.

"I've fixed him!" he answered with an expressive wink.

Passing through the custom house we were made happy by the information that it had been decided to attach a passenger coach to the special mail train to oblige the passengers who wished to go to London without delay. The train was made up then, so we concluded to get into our car and try to warm up.

A porter took my bag and another man in uniform drew forth an enormous key with which he unlocked the door in the side of the car instead of the end, as in America. I managed to compass the uncomfortable long step to the door and striking my toe against some projection in the floor, went most ungracefully and unceremoniously on to the seat.

My escort after giving some order to the porter went out to see about my ticket, so I took a survey of an English railway compartment. The little square in which I sat looked like a hotel omnibus and was about as comfortable. The two red leather seats in it run across the car, one backing the engine, the other backing the rear of the train. There was a door on either side and one could hardly have told that there was a dingy lamp there to cast a light on the scene had not the odor from it been so loud. I carefully lifted the rug that covered the thing I had fallen over, curious to see what could be so necessary to an English railway carriage as to occupy such a prominent position. I found a harmless object that looked like a bar of iron and had just dropped the rug in place when the door opened and the porter, catching the iron at one end, pulled it out, replacing it with another like it in shape and size.

"Put your feet on the foot warmer and get warm, Miss," he said, and I mechanically did as he advised.

My escort returned soon after, followed by a porter who carried a large basket which he put in our carriage. The guard came afterwards and took our tickets. Pasting a slip of paper on the window, which backwards looked like "etavirP," he went out and locked the door.

"How should we get out if the train ran the track?" I asked, not half liking the idea of being locked in a box like an animal in a freight train.

"Trains never run off the track in England," was the quiet, satisfied answer.

"Too slow for that," I said teasingly, which only provoked a gentle inquiry as to whether I wanted anything to eat.

With a newspaper spread over our laps for a table-cloth, we brought out what the basket contained and put in our time eating and chatting about my journey until the train reached London.

As no train was expected at that hour, Waterloo Station was almost deserted. It was some little time after we stopped before the guard unlocked the door of our compartment and released us. Our few fellow-passengers were just about starting off in shabby cabs when we alighted. Once again we called goodbye and good wishes to each other, and then I found myself in a four-wheeled cab, facing a young Englishman who had come to meet us and who was glibly telling us the latest news.

I don't know at what hour we arrived, but my companions told me that it was daylight. I should not have known it. A gray, misty fog hung like a ghostly pall over the city. I always liked fog, it lends such a soft, beautifying light to things that otherwise in the broad glare of day would be rude and commonplace.

"How are these streets compared with those of New York?" was the first question that broke the silence after our leaving the station.

"They are not bad," I said with a patronizing air, thinking shamefacedly of the dreadful streets of New York, although determined to hear no word against them.

Westminster Abbey and the Houses of Parliament were pointed out to me, and the Thames, across which we drove. I felt that I was taking what might be called a bird's-eye view of London. A great many foreigners have taken views in the same rapid way of America, and afterwards gone home and written books about America, Americans, and Americanisms.

We drove first to the London office of the New York *World*. After receiving the cables that were waiting for my arrival, I started for the American Legation to get a passport as I had been instructed by cable.

Mr. McCormick, Secretary of the Legation, came into the room immediately after our arrival, and after welcoming and congratulating me on the successful termination of the first portion of my trip, sat down and wrote out a passport.

My escort was asked to go into another part of the room until the representative could ask me an important question. I had never required a passport before, and I felt a nervous curiosity to know what secrets were connected with such proceedings.

"There is one question all women dread to answer, and as very few will give a truthful reply, I will ask you to swear to the rest first and fill in the other question afterwards, unless you have no hesitancy in telling me your age."

"Oh, certainly," I laughed. "I will tell you my age, swear to it, too, and I am not afraid; my companion may come out of the corner."

"What is the color of your eyes?" he asked.

"Green," I said indifferently.

He was inclined to doubt it at first, but after a little inspection, both the gentlemen accepted my verdict as correct.

It was only a few seconds until we were whirling through the streets of London again. This time we went to the office of the Peninsular and Oriental Steamship Company, where I bought tickets that would cover at least half of my journey. A few moments again and we were driving rapidly to the Charing Cross station.

I was faint for food, and while my companion dismissed the cab and secured tickets, I ordered the only thing on the Charing Cross bill of fare that was prepared, so when he returned, his breakfast was ready for him. It was only ham and eggs, and coffee, but what we got of it was delicious. I know we did not get much, and when we were interrupted by the announcement that our train was starting, I stopped long enough to take another drink of coffee and then had to run down the platform to catch the train.

There is nothing like plenty of food to preserve health. I know that cup of coffee saved me from a headache that day. I had been shaking with the cold as we made our hurried drive through London, and my head was so dizzy at times that I hardly knew whether the earth had a chill or my brains were attending a ball. When I got comfortable seated in the train I began to feel warmer and more stable.

The train moved off at an easy-going speed, and the very jog of it lulled me into a state of languor.

"I want you to see the scenery along here; it is beautiful," my companion said, but I lazily thought, "What is scenery compared with sleep when one has not seen bed for over twenty-four hours?" so I said to him, very crossly:

"Don't you think you would better take a nap? You have not had any sleep for so long and you will be up so late to-night, that, really, I think for the sake of your health you would better sleep now."

"And you?" he asked with a teasing smile. I had been up even longer.

"Well, I confess, I was saying one word for you and two for myself," I replied, with a laugh that put us at ease on the subject.

"Honestly, now, I care very little for scenery when I am so sleepy," I said apologetically. "Those English farm houses are charming and the daisy-dotted meadows (I had not the faintest conception as to whether there were daisies in them or not), are only equaled by those I have seen in Kansas, but if you will excuse me?—" and I was in the land that joins the land of death.

I slept an easy, happy sleep, filled with dreams of home until I was waked by the train stopping.

"We change for the boat here," my companion said catching up our bags and rugs, which he hauled to a porter.

A little walk down to the pier brought us to the place where a boat was waiting. Some people were getting off the boat, but a larger number stood idly about waiting for it to move off.

The air was very cold and chilly, but still I preferred the deck to the close, musty-smelling cabin beneath. Two English women also remained on deck. I was much amused at the conversation they held with some friends who had accompanied them to the boat, and now stood on the wharf. One would have supposed, by hearing the conversation that they had only that instant met and having no time to spend together, were forced to make all further arrangements on the spot.

"You will come over to-morrow, now don't forget," the young woman on the boat called out.

"I won't forget. Are you certain that you have everything with you?" the one on the wharf called back.

"Look after Fido. Give him that compound in the morning if there is no appearance of improvement," the first one said.

"You will meet me to-morrow?" said number two on shore.

"Oh yes; don't forget to come," was the reply, and as the boat moved out they both talked at once until we were quite a distance off, then simultaneously the one turned to her chair and the other turned around and walked rapidly away from the wharf.

There has been so much written and told about the English Channel, that one is inclined to think of it as a stream of horrors. It is also affirmed that even hardy sailors bring up the past when crossing over it, so I naturally felt that my time would come.

All the passengers must have been familiar with the history of the channel, for I saw everyone trying all the known preventives of seasickness. The women assumed reclining positions and the men sought the bar.

I remained on deck and watched the sea-gulls, or what I thought were these useful birds—useful for millinery purposes—and froze my nose. It was bitterly cold, but I found the cold bracing until we anchored at Boulogne, France. Then I had a chill.

At the end of this desolate pier, where boats anchor and where trains start, is a small, dingy restaurant. While a little English sailor, who always dropped his h's and never forgot his "sir," took charge of our bags and went to secure accommodations for us in the outgoing train, we followed the other passengers into the restaurant to get something warm to eat.

I was in France now, and I began to wonder now what would have been my fate if I had been alone as I had expected. I knew my companion spoke French, the language that all the people about us were speaking, so I felt perfectly easy on that score as long as he was with me.

We took our places at the table and he began to order in French. The waiter looked blankly at him until, at last, more in a spirit of fun than anything else, I suggested that he give the order in English. The waiter glanced at me with a smile and answered in English.

We traveled from Boulogne to Amiens in a compartment with an English couple and a Frenchman. There was one foot-warmer and the day was cold. We all tried to put our feet on the one foot-warmer and the result was embarrassing. The Frenchman sat facing me and as I was conscious of having tramped on someone's toes, and as he looked at me angrily all the time above the edge of his newspaper, I had a guilty feeling of knowing whose toes had been tramped on.

During this trip I tried to solve the reason for the popularity of these ancient, incommodious railway carriages. I very shortly decided that while they may be suitable for countries where little traveling is done, they would be thoroughly useless in thinly populated countries where people think less of traveling 3,000 miles than they do about their dinner. I also decided that the reason why we think nothing of starting out on long trips, is because our comfort is so well looked after, that living on a first-class railway train is as comfortable as living at a first-class hotel. The English railway carriages are wretchedly heated. One's feet will be burning on the foot-warmer while one's back will be freezing in the cold air above. If one should be taken suddenly ill in an English railway compartment, it would be a very serious matter.

Still, I can picture conditions under which these ancient railway carriages might be agreeable, but they are not such as would induce a traveler to prefer them to those built on the American model.

NELLIE BLY

Supposing one had the measles or a black eye, then a compartment in a railway carriage, made private by a tip to the porter, would be very consoling.

Supposing one was newly wed and was bubbling over in ecstacy of joy, then give one an English railway compartment, where two just made one can be secluded from the eyes of a cold, sneering public, who are just as great fools under the same conditions, although they would deny it if one told them so.

But talk about privacy! If it is privacy the English desire so much, they should adopt our American trains, for there is no privacy like that to be found in a large car filled with strangers. Everybody has, and keeps his own place. There is no sitting for hours, as is often the case in English trains, face to face and knees to knees with a stranger, offensive or otherwise, as he may chance to be.

Then too, did the English railway carriage make me understand why English girls need chaperones. It would make any American woman shudder with all her boasted self-reliance, to think of sending her daughter alone on a trip, even of a few hours' duration, where there was every possibility that during those hours she would be locked in a compartment with a stranger.

Small wonder the American girl is fearless. She has not been used to so called private compartments in English railway carriages, but to large crowds, and every individual that helps to swell that crowd is to her a protector. When mothers teach their daughters that there is safety in numbers, and that numbers are the body-guard that shield all woman-kind, then chaperones will be a thing of the past, and women will be nobler and better.

As I was pondering over this subject, the train pulled into a station and stopped. My escort looking out, informed me that we were at Amiens. We were securely locked in, however, and began to think that we would be carried past, when my companion managed to get his head out of the window and shouted for the guard to come to our release. Freed at last, we stepped out on the platform at Amiens.

IV

JULES VERNE AT HOME

M. Jules Verne and Mme. Verne, accompanied by Mr. R. H. Sherard, a Paris journalist, stood on the platform waiting our arrival.

When I saw them I felt as any other woman would have done under the same circumstances. I wondered if my face was travel-stained, and if my hair was tossed. I thought regretfully, had I been traveling on an American train, I should have been able to make my toilet *en route*, so that when I stepped off at Amiens and faced the famous novelist and his charming wife, I would have been as trim and tidy as I would had I been receiving them in my own home.

There was little time for regret. They were advancing towards us, and in another second I had forgotten my untidiness in the cordial welcome they gave me. Jules Verne's bright eyes beamed on me with interest and kindliness, and Mme. Verne greeted me with the cordiality of a cherished friend. There were no stiff formalities to freeze the kindness in all our hearts, but a cordiality expressed with such charming grace that before I had been many minutes in their company, they had won my everlasting respect and devotion.

M. Verne led the way to the carriages which waited our coming. Mme. Verne walked closely by my side, glancing occasionally at me with a smile, which said in the language of the eye, the common language of the whole animal world, alike plain to man and beast:

"I am glad to greet you, and I regret we cannot speak together." M. Verne gracefully helped Mme. Verne and myself into a coupé, while he entered a carriage with the two other gentlemen. I felt very awkward at being left alone with Mme. Verne, as I was altogether unable to speak to her.

Her knowledge of the English language consisted of "No" and my French vocabulary consisted of "Oui," so our conversation was limited to a few apologetic and friendly smiles interluded with an occasional pressure of the hand. Indeed, Mme. Verne is a most charming woman, and even in this awkward position she made everything go most gracefully.

It was early evening. As we drove through the streets of Amiens I got a flying glimpse of bright shops, a pretty park, and numerous nurse maids pushing baby carriages about.

When our carriage stopped I got out and gave my hand to Mme. Verne to help her alight. We stood on a wide, smooth pavement, before a high stone wall, over the top of which I could see the peaked outlines of the house.

M. Verne was not long behind us. He hurried up to where we were standing and opened a door in the wall. Stepping in I found myself in a small, smoothly paved court-yard, the wall making two sides and the house forming the square.

A large, black shaggy dog came bounding forward to greet me. He jumped up against me, his soft eyes overflowing with affection, and though I love dogs and especially appreciated this one's loving welcome, still I feared that his lavish display of it would undermine my dignity by bringing me to my knees at the very threshold of the home of the famous Frenchman.

M. Verne evidently understood my plight, for he spoke shortly to the dog, who, with a pathetic droop of his tail, went off to think it out alone.

We went up a flight of marble steps across the tiled floor of a beautiful little conservatory that was not packed with flowers but was filled with a display just generous enough to allow one to see and appreciate the beauty of the different plants. Mme. Verne led the way into a large sitting-room that was dusky with the early shade of a wintry evening. With her own hands she touched a match to the pile of dry wood that lay in the wide open fireplace.

Meanwhile M. Verne urged us to remove our outer wrappings. Before this was done a bright fire was crackling in the grate, throwing a soft, warm light over the dark room. Mme. Verne led me to a chair close by the mantel, and when I was seated she took the chair opposite. Cheered by the warmth I looked quietly on the scene before me.

The room was large and the hangings and paintings and soft velvet rug, which left visible but a border of polished hard wood, were richly dark. On the mantel, which towered above Mme. Verne's head, were some fine pieces of statuary in bronze and, as the fire gave frequent bright flashes as the flames greedily caught fresh wood, I could see another bronze piece on a pedestal in a corner. All the chairs artistically upholstered in brocaded silks, were luxuriously easy. Beginning at either side of the mantel they were placed in a semi-circle around the fire, which was only broken by a little table that held several tall silver candlesticks.

A fine white Angora cat came rubbing up against my knee, then seeing its charming mistress on the opposite side, went to her and boldly crawled up in her lap as if assured of a cordial welcome.

Next to me in this semi-circle sat Mr. Sherard. M. Jules Verne was next to Mr. Sherard. He sat forward on the edge of his chair, his snow-white hair rather long and heavy, was standing up in artistic disorder; his full beard, rivaling his hair in snowiness, hid the lower part of his face and the brilliancy of his bright eyes that were overshadowed with heavy white brows, and the rapidity of his speech and the quick movements of his firm white hands all bespoke energy—life—with enthusiasm.

The London correspondent sat next to Jules Verne. With a smile on her soft rosy lips, Mme. Verne sat nursing the cat which she stroked methodically with a dainty, white hand, while her luminous black eyes moved alternately between her husband and myself.

She was the most charming figure in that group around the wood fire. Imagine a youthful face with a spotless complexion, crowned with the whitest hair, dressed in smooth, soft folds on the top of a dainty head that is most beautifully poised on a pair of plump shoulders. Add to this face pretty red lips, that opened disclose a row of lovely teeth, and large, bewitching black eyes, and you have but a faint picture of the beauty of Mme. Verne.

This day when she met me she wore a sealskin jacket and carried a muff, and on her white head was a small black velvet bonnet. On taking her wraps off in the house I saw she wore a watered-silk skirt, laid in side plaits in the front with a full straight black drapery, that was very becoming to her short, plump figure. The bodice was of black silk velvet.

Mme. Verne is, I should judge, not more than five feet two in height; M. Verne about five feet five. M. Verne spoke in a short, rapid way, and Mr. Sherard in an attractive, lazy voice translated what was said for my benefit.

"Has M. Verne ever been to America?" I asked.

"Yes, once;" the answer came translated to me. "For a few days only, during which time I saw Niagara. I have always longed to return, but the state of my health prevents my taking any long journeys. I try to keep a knowledge of everything that is going on in America and greatly appreciate the hundreds of letters I receive yearly from Americans who read my books. There is one man in California who has been writing to me for years. He writes all the news about his family and home and country as if I were a friend and yet we have never met. He has urged me to come to America as his guest. I know of nothing that I long to do more than to see your land from New York to San Francisco."

"How did you get the idea for your novel, 'Around the World in Eighty Days?'" I asked.

"I got it from a newspaper," was his reply. "I took up a copy of *Le Siécle* one morning, and found in it a discussion and some calculations showing that the journey around the world might be done in eighty days. The idea pleased me, and while thinking it over it struck me that in their calculations they had not called into account the difference in the meridians and I thought what a denouement such a thing would make in a novel, so I went to work to write one. Had it not been for the denouement I don't think that I should ever have written the book."

"I used to keep a yacht, and then I traveled all over the world studying localities; then I wrote from actual observation. Now, since my health confines me to my home, I am forced to read up descriptions and geographies."

M. Verne asked me what my line of travel was to be, and I was very happy to speak one thing that he could understand, so I told him.

"My line of travel is from New York to London, then Calais, Brindisi, Port Said, Ismailia, Suez, Aden, Colombo, Penang, Singapore, Hong Kong, Yokohama, San Francisco, New York."

"Why do you not go to Bombay as my hero Phileas Fogg did?" M. Verne asked.

"Because I am more anxious to save time than a young widow," I answered.

"You may save a young widower before you return," M. Verne said with a smile.

I smiled with a superior knowledge, as women, fancy free, always will at such insinuations.

I looked at the watch on my wrist and saw that my time was getting short. There was only one train that I could take from here to Calais, and if I missed it I might just as well return to New York by the way I came, for the loss of that train meant one week's delay.

"If M. Verne would not consider it impertinent I should like to see his study before I go," I said at last.

He said he was only too happy to show it me, and even as my request was translated Mme. Verne sprang to her feet and lighted one of the tall wax candles.

She started with the quick, springy step of a girl to lead the way. M. Verne, who walks with a slight limp, the result of a wound, followed, and we brought up the rear. We went through the conservatory to a small room up through which was a winding stair, or, more properly speaking, a spiral stair-case. Mme. Verne paused at every curve to light the gas.

Up at the top of the house and along a hall that corresponded in shape to the conservatory below, M. Verne went, Mme. Verne stopping to light the gas in the hall. He opened a door that led off the hall and I stepped inside after him.

I was astonished. I had expected, judging from the rest of the house, that M. Verne's study would be a room of ample proportions and richly furnished. I had read so many descriptions of the studies of famous authors, and have dwelt with something akin to envy (our space is so limited and expensive in New York) on the ample room, the beautiful hand-carved desks filled with costly trinkets, the rare etchings and paintings that covered the walls, the rich hangings, and, I will confess it, I have thought it small wonder that amid such surroundings authors were able to dream fancies that brought them fame.

But when I stood in M. Verne's study I was speechless with surprise. He opened a latticed window, the only window in the room, and Mme. Verne, hurrying in after us, lighted the gas jet that was fastened above a low mantel.

The room was very small; even my little den at home was almost as large. It was also very modest and bare. Before the window was a flat-topped desk. The usual litter that accompanies and fills the desks of most literary persons was conspicuously absent, and the waste-basket that is usually filled to overflowing with what one very often considers their most brilliant productions, in this case held but a few little scraps.

On the desk was a neat little pile of white paper, probably 8x10 in size. It was part of the manuscript of a novel that M. Verne is engaged on at present. I eagerly accepted the manuscript when he handed it to me, and when I looked at the neat penmanship, so neat in fact that had I not known it was prose I should have thought it was the work of a poet, I was more impressed than ever with the extreme tidiness of this French author. In several places he had most effectually blotted out something that he had written, but there was no interlining, which gave me the idea that M. Verne always improved his work by taking out superfluous things and never by adding.

One bottle of ink and one penholder was all that shared the desk with the manuscript. There was but one chair in the room, and it stood before the desk. The only other piece of furniture was a broad, low couch in the corner, and here in this room with these meagre surroundings, Jules Verne has written the books that have brought him everlasting fame.

I leaned over the desk and looked out of the little latticed window which he had thrown open. I could see through the dusk the spire of a cathedral in the distance, while stretching down beneath me was a park, beyond which I saw the entrance to a railway tunnel that goes under M. Verne's house, and through which many Americans travel every year, on their way to Paris.

Leading off from the study, is an enormous library. The large room is completely lined with cases from ceiling to floor, and these glass-doored cases are packed with handsomely bound books which must be worth a fortune.

While we were examining the wealth of literature that was there before us, M. Verne got an idea. Taking up a candle and asking us to follow, he went out into the hall; stopping before a large map that hung there, holding up with one hand the candle, he pointed out to us several blue marks. Before his words were translated to me, I understood that on this map he had, with a blue pencil, traced out the course of his hero, Phileas Fogg, before he started him in fiction to travel around the world in eighty days. With a pencil he marked on the map, as we grouped about him, the places where my line of travel differed from that of Phileas Fogg.

Our steps lagged as we descended the winding stair again. It had come time to take farewell, and I felt as if I was separating from friends. Down in the room where we had been before, we found wine and biscuit on the little table, and M. Jules Verne explained that, contrary to his regular rules, he intended to take a glass of wine, that we might have the pleasure of drinking together to the success of my strange undertaking.

They clinked their glasses with wine, and wished me "God speed."

"If you do it in seventy-nine days, I shall applaud with both hands," Jules Verne said, and then I knew he doubted the possibility of my doing it in seventy-five, as I had promised. In compliment to me, he endeavored to speak to me in English, and did succeed in saying, as his glass tipped mine:

"Good luck, Nellie Bly."

Mme. Verne was not going to be outdone by her gallant husband in showing kindness to me. She told Mr. Sherard that she would like to kiss me good-bye, and when he translated her kind request, he added that it was a great honor in France, for a woman to ask to kiss a stranger.

I was little used to such formalities, or familiarities, as one may deem them, but still I had not one thought of refusing such delicate attention, so I gave her my hand and inclined my head, for I am taller than she, and she kissed me gently and affectionately on either cheek. Then she put up her pretty face for me to kiss. I stifled a strong inclination to kiss her on the lips, they were so sweet and red, and show her how we do it in America. My mischievousness often plays havoc with my dignity, but for once I was able to restrain myself, and kissed her softly after her own fashion.

With uncovered heads, and despite our protestations, they followed us out into the cold court-yard, and as far as I could see I saw them standing at the gate waving farewell to me, the brisk winds tossing their white hair.

V

ON TO BRINDISI

When M. and Mme. Verne were no longer visible, my thoughts turned to my trip. I feared that the enjoyment of my visit to their home had jeopardized the success of my tour.

The driver had been told to make the best speed back to the station, but the carriage seemed to be rolling along so quietly that I could not rest until it was urged again upon the coachman to reach the station in the shortest possible time.

Some few moments after we reached there the train came in. Bidding a hearty good-bye to Mr. Sherard, I started again on my tour of the world, and the visit to Jules Verne was a thing of the past. I had gone without sleep and rest; I had traveled many miles out of my way for the privilege of meeting M. and Mme. Verne, and I felt that if I had gone around the world for that pleasure, I should not have considered the price too high.

The train which carried us to Calais is, I infer from what I have heard, the pride of France. It is called the Club train, and is built on the plan of the vestibule trains in America. The carriages are so narrow, that after having been accustomed to wide ones, the Club train seems like a toy.

I have been curious to know why this train is called the Club train. I had a foolish idea at first that it was the private property of some club, run for the special benefit of its members, and I felt some hesitancy about traveling on a train devoted to the use of men. However, the presence of a number of women put me at ease, and though I made many inquiries about the train, all I could learn was that it was considered quite the finest equipped train in Europe.

The car in which we sat, as I said before, contained some women, and was besides liberally filled with men passengers. Shortly after we left Amiens, a porter announced that dinner was served in a front car. Everybody at once filed out and into the dining car. I have thought since that probably the train carried two dining cars, because the dinner, and an excellent one it proved to be, was served *table d'hôte*, and there seemed to be accommodations for all.

After we had our cheese and salad, we returned to our drawing-room car, where we were served with coffee, the men having the privilege of smoking with it. I thought this manner of serving coffee a very pleasing one, quite an improvement on our own system, and quite worthy of adoption.

When I reached Calais, I found that I had two hours and more to spend in waiting. The train that I intended to take for Brindisi is a weekly mail train that runs to accommodate the mails and not passengers. It starts originally from London, at eight o'clock Friday evening of each week. The rule is that the persons desiring to travel on it must buy their tickets twenty-four hours in advance of the time of its departure. The mail and passengers are carried across the channel, and the train leaves Calais at 1.30 in the morning.

There are pleasanter places in the world to waste time in than Calais. I walked down along the pier and looked at the light-house, which I am told is one of the most perfect in the world, throwing its light farther away than any other. It is a revolving light, and it throws out long rays that seem so little above our heads that I found myself dodging to avoid being struck. Of course, that was purely imaginary on my part, for the rays are just the opposite to being near the ground, but they spread between the ground and the sky like the laths of an unfinished partition. I wonder if the people of Calais ever saw the moon and stars.

There is a very fine railway station built near the end of the pier. It is of generous size, but seemed, as far as I could judge, at this hour of the night, quite empty. There is a smoothly tiled enclosed promenade on the side of the station facing the pier that I should say would prove quite an attraction and comfort for passengers who were forced to wait in that place.

My escort took me into the restaurant where we found something to eat, which was served by a French waiter who could speak some English and understand more. When it was announced that the boat from England was in we went out and saw the be-bundled and be-baggaged passengers come ashore and go to the train which was waiting alongside. One thousand bags of mail were quickly transferred to the train, and then I bade my escort good-bye, and was shortly speeding away from Calais.

There is but one passenger coach on this train. It is a Pullman Palace sleeping-car with accommodations for twenty-two passengers, but it is the rule never to carry more than twenty-one, one berth being occupied by the guard.

The next morning, having nothing else to occupy my time, I thought that I would see what my traveling companions looked like. I had shared the stateroom at the extreme end of the car with a pretty English girl who had the rosiest cheeks and the greatest wealth of golden brown hair I ever saw. She was going with her father, an invalid, to Egypt, to spend the winter and spring months. She was an early riser, and before I was awake had gotten up and joined her father in the other part of the car.

When I went out so as to give the porter an opportunity to make up my stateroom, I was surprised at the strange appearance of the interior of the car. All the head and foot boards were left in place, giving the impression that the coach was divided into a series of small boxes. Some of the passengers were drinking, some were playing cards, and all were smoking until the air was stifling. I never object to cigar smoke when there is some little ventilation, but when it gets so thick that one feels as if it is molasses instead of air that one is inhaling, then I mildly protest. It was soon this occasion, and I wonder what would be the result in our land of boasted freedom if a Pullman car should be put to such purposes. I concluded it is due to this freedom that we do not suffer from such things. Women travelers in America command as much consideration as men.

I walked down the car looking in the "boxes" only to find them all occupied by unsocial looking men. When I reached the middle of the car my little English room-mate, who was sitting with her father, saw me and kindly asked me to sit down with them.

Her father I remember as a cultured, broad-minded man, with a sense of humor that helped me to hear with less dread the racking cough that frequently stopped all speech and shook his thin frame as though he had the ague.

"Father," the little English girl said in a clear, musical voice, "the clergyman sent you his large prayer-book just before our departure, and I put it in your bag."

"My daughter is very thoughtful," he said to me, then turning to her he added, with a smile in his eye, "Please take the first opportunity to return the prayer-book to the clergyman, and tell him, with my compliments, that he might have saved himself that trouble; that I was grieved to deprive him of his book for so long."

The young girl's face settled into a look that spoke disapproval of her father's words, and a determination not to return the prayer-book. She held, clasped to her breast. a large prayer-book, and when her father jokingly told her she had bought the largest one she could find, which he looked on as wasting valuable packing space, when she could have carried a small one that would have been of as much service, I was actually startled by the hard, determined light on her face. In everything else she was the sweetest, most gentle girl I ever met, but her religion was of the hard, uncompromising kind, that condemns everything, forgives nothing, and swears the heathen is forever damned because he was not born to know the religion of her belief.

She spent all the afternoon trying to implant the seeds of her faith in my mind, and I listened, thinking from her words that if she was not the original Catherine Elsmere, she at least could not be more like that interesting character.

For the first day food was taken on the train at different stations, and the conductor, or guard, as they called him, served it to the passengers. A dining car was attached in the evening but I was informed by the women that it was not exactly the thing for us to eat in a public car with men, so we continued to be served in our state rooms.

I might have seen more while traveling through France if the car windows had been clean. From their appearance I judged that they had never been washed. We did not make many stops. The only purpose of stopping was for coal or water, as passengers are not taken on or off this train between Calais and Brindisi.

In the course of the afternoon we passed some high and picturesque mountains that were covered with a white frost. I found that even wearing my ulster and wrapped in a rug I was none too warm. About eight o'clock in the morning we reached Modena. The baggage was examined there and all the passengers were notified in advance to be prepared to get out and unlock the boxes that belonged to them. The conductor asked me several times if I was quite certain that I had no more than the handbag with me, telling me at the same time if any boxes were found locked, with no owner to open them, they would be detained by the custom inspectors. When partly assured that I had no trunks he said that it was not necessary to get out with my hand-bag, as no one would think it necessary to examine it.

Half an hour later we were in Italy. I was anxiously waiting to see that balmy, sunny land, but though I pressed my face close to the frosty window pane bleak night denied me even one glimpse of sunny Italy and its dusky people. I went to bed early. It was so very cold that I could not keep warm out of bed, and I cannot say that I got much warmer in bed. The berths were provided with only one blanket each. I piled all my clothing on the berth and spent half the night lying awake thinking how fortunate the passengers were the week previous on this train. Just in the very same place that we were traveling through Italian bandits had attacked the train and I thought, with regretful envy, if the passengers then felt the scarcity of blankets they at least had some excitement to make their blood circulate.

When I got awake in the morning I hastily threw up the window shade and eagerly looked out. I fell back in surprise, wondering, if for once in my life I had made a mistake and waked up early. I could not see any more than I had the night before on account of a heavy gray fog that completely hid everything more than a yard away. Looking at the watch on my wrist I found that it was ten o'clock, so I dressed with some haste determined to find the guard and demand an explanation of him.

"It is a most extraordinary thing," he said to me; "I never saw such a fog in Italy before."

There was nothing for it except to sit quietly counting the days I had been away from New York; subtracting them from the number that must elapse before my return. When this grew monotonous I carefully thought over the advisability of trying to introduce brown uniforms for railroad employees in the United States. I thought with wearied frenzy of the universal employment of navy-blue uniforms in America, and I turned with rest to the neat brown uniforms brightened with a touching of gold braid on the collars and cuffs, that adorned the conductor and porter of the India mail.

But even this subject would not fill the day, so I began to notice the difference between the whistles employed on these engines and those at home. There was no deafening, ear-racking blast from these, but plaintive sounds, pitched in a high key that was very soprano indeed, compared with our bass whistles.

I noticed in Italy, as in all the other countries where I found railroads, that trains are started by a blast from a tin horn—horns such as those that take conspicuous places in political campaigns once every four years, succeeding, by the aid of enthusiastic campaigners, in making night hideous for several months preceding the election.

In most cases these horn-blowers seemed to be located at the station, but in France and Italy they occupied the front platform of a coach, and I noticed, with amusement, that the tin horns were chained to them.

All day I traveled through Italy—sunny Italy, along the Adriatic Sea. The fog still hung in a heavy cloud over the earth, and only once did I get a glimpse of the land I had heard so much about. It was evening, just at the hour of sunset, when we stopped at some station. I went out on the platform, and the fog seemed to lift for an instant, and I saw on one side a beautiful beach and a smooth bay dotted with boats bearing oddly-shaped and brightly-colored sails, which somehow looked to me like mammoth butterflies, dipping, dipping about in search of honey. Most of the sails were red, and as the sun kissed them with renewed warmth, just before leaving us in darkness, the sails looked as if they were composed of brilliant fire.

A high rugged mountain was on the other side of the train. It made me feel dizzy to look at the white buildings perched on the perpendicular side. I noticed the road that went in a winding line up the hill had been built with a wall on the ocean side; still I thought I would not care to travel up it.

I got out for a few minutes at the next station where we stopped to take our dinners. I walked into a restaurant to look about. It was very neat and attractive. Just as I stepped inside a little girl with wonderful large black eyes and enormous gold hoop-rings in her ears, ran forward to me with the fearless boldness of a child. I touched her pretty black hair, and then naturally felt in my pocket for something to give her. Just as I drew forth a large copper coin—the less the value of a coin generally, the larger its size—a small man with a delicately refined face, flashing black eyes, wide expanse of white shirt front, broken by a brilliant diamond, came up and spoke to the baby. In the way she drew back from me, although her little hand had been stretched out expectantly before, I knew he had told her not to accept anything from me.

I felt on first impulse like boxing his ears, he was so tiny and impudent. The guard coming in search of me, found us at this critical moment.

"You have insulted him," he said to me, as if I was not conscious of it! "The Italians are the poorest and proudest people on earth. They hate the English."

"I am an American," I said bluntly and abruptly. At this a waiter who had been standing close by apparently not listening, but catching every word just the same, came up and spoke to me in English. Then I determined to remedy the fault I had committed, but nevertheless I had a dogged determination that the child should yet take the coin.

"What a beautiful restaurant!" I exclaimed. "I am passing hurriedly through Italy and in my desire to see, judging from the samples of good cooking I have had *en route*, Italian eating houses are excellent. I hope I have not put you to any inconvenience. I almost forgot the restaurant when I saw that lovely baby. What exquisitely beautiful eyes! Exactly the same as her father's, at least I judge from the similarity of their eyes that he is her father, though he looks so young."

The waiter smiled and bowed and translated. I knew he would, and that is why I said it all. Then the little man's pride melted away, and a smile replaced the frown on his face. He spoke to the baby who came up and shook hands with me. I gave her the coin and our peace was sealed. Then the little father brought forth a bottle of wine, and with the most cordial smiles and friendliest words, begged me to accept it. I did not intend to be out-done, so I told the waiter that I must take some wine with me, insisted on paying for it, and with low bows and sweet smiles we took leave of one another, and I rushed after the guard to the train, boarding it just as the horn blew for it to continue on its way.

We arrived at Brindisi two hours late. When the train stopped, our car was surrounded with men wanting to carry us as well as our baggage to the boats. Their making no mention of hotels led me to wonder if people always passed through Brindisi without stopping. All these men spoke English very well, but the guard said he would get one omnibus and escort the English women, the invalid man and his daughter, and myself to our boats, and would see that we were not charged more than the right fare.

We drove first to the boat bound for Alexandria, where we took leave of my room-mate, and her father. Then we drove to the boat that we expected to sail on.

I alighted from the omnibus, and followed my companions up the gang plank. I dreaded meeting English people with their much-talked-of prejudices, as I knew I would shortly have to do. I was earnestly hoping that everybody would be in bed. As it was after one in the morning, I hardly expected the trial of facing them at once. The crowds of men on the deck dispelled my fond hope. I think every man on board that boat was up waiting to see the new passengers. They must have felt but illy paid for their loss of sleep, for besides the men who came on board, there were only the two large English women and my own plain, uninteresting self.

These women were more helpless than I. As they were among their own people, I waited for them to take the lead; but after we had stood at the foot of the stairs for some time, gazed at by the passengers, and no one came forward to attend to our wants, which were few and simple, I gently asked if that was the usual manner of receiving passengers on English boats.

"It is strange, very strange. A steward, or some one should come to our assistance," was all they could say.

At last a man came down below, and as he looked as if he was in some way connected with the boat, I ventured to stop him and inquire if it was expecting too much to ask if we might have a steward to show us to our cabins. He said there should be some about, and began lustily to call for one. Even this brought no one to us, and as he started to find one himself, I started in the opposite direction.

Among the crowd that stood about was but one man that dared to speak without waiting for an introduction before he could be commonly polite.

"You will find the purser in his office the first door to the left there," he said; and I went that way, followed by the guard from the train.

Sitting in the office was the purser and a man I supposed to be the doctor. I gave my ticket and a letter I had been given at the P. & O. office in London, to the purser. This letter requested that the commanders and pursers of all the P. & O. boats on which I traveled should give me all the care and attention it was in their power as such officers to bestow.

After leisurely reading the letter, the purser very carelessly turned around and told me the number of my cabin. I asked for a steward to show me the way, but he replied that there did not seen to be any about, that the cabin was on the port side, and with this meagre information, he impolitely turned his back and busied himself with some papers on the desk before him.

The train guard who still stood by my side, said he would help me find the cabin. After a little search, we did find it. I opened the door and stepped in, and the sight that met my eyes both amused me and dismayed me. At the opening of the door, two bushy heads were stuck out of the two lower berths, and two high pitched voices exclaimed simultaneously with a vexed intonation, "Oh!" I looked at the band-boxes, boots, hand bags, gowns and the upper berth that was also filled with clothes, and I echoed their "Oh!" in a little different tone and retired.

I returned to the purser and told him I could not sleep in an upper berth, and would not occupy a cabin with two other women. After looking again over the letter I had brought him, as if to see how much weight he should give it, he referred me to another cabin. This time a steward made his appearance and he took the part of an escort.

I found a pretty girl in that cabin, who lifted her head anxiously, and then gave me a friendly smile when I entered. I put my bag down and returned to the guard who was waiting to take me to the cable office. I stopped to ask the purser if I had time to make the trip, to which he replied in the affirmative, with the proviso, "If you hurry." The two women who had traveled with me from Calais, had by this time found their way to the purser's office, and I heard them telling that they had come away from home and left their purse and tickets lying on the table in the sitting-room, they had started in such a rush!

The guard took me down the gang plank, and along several dark streets. At last, coming to a building where a door stood open, he stopped and I followed him in. The room in which we stood was perfectly bare and lighted by a lamp whose chimney was badly smoked. The only things in the room were two stationary desks. On the one lay a piece of blank paper before an ancient ink well and a much used pen.

I thought that everybody had retired for the night, and the cable would have to wait until I reached the next port, until the guard explained to me that it was customary to ring for the operator, who would get up and attend to the message for me. Suiting the action to the words, the guard pulled at a knob near a small closed window, much like a postage stamp window. The bell made quite a clatter, still I had begun to think that hopeless, when the window opened with a clink, and a head appeared at the opening. The guard spoke in Italian, but hearing me speak English, the operator replied in the same language.

I told him I wanted to send a cable to New York. He asked me where New York was! I explained as best I could; then he brought out a lot of books, through which he searched first, to know by which line he could send the message; at least, so he explained; then what it would cost. The whole thing was so new and amusing to me that I forgot all about the departure of the boat until we had finished the business and stepped outside.

A whistle blew long and warningly. I looked at the guard, the guard looked at me. It was too dark to see each other, but I know our faces were the picture of dismay. My heart stopped beating and I thought with emotions akin to horror, "My boat was gone—and with it my limited wardrobe!"

"Can you run?" the guard asked in a husky voice. I said I could, and he taking a close grasp of my hand, we started down the dark street with a speed that would have startled a deer. Down the dark streets, past astonished watchmen and late pedestrians, until a sudden bend brought us in full view of my ship still in port. The boat for Alexandria had gone, but I was saved.

VI

AN AMERICAN HEIRESS

I had not been asleep long, it seemed to me, until I waked to find myself standing upright beside my berth. It required but a second, a glance at my drenched self, and the sounds of vigorous scrubbing on the deck above to explain the cause of my being out of bed before I knew it. I had gone to sleep with the port-hole open, and as my berth was just beneath it, I received the full force of the scrub-water as it came pouring over the sides. I managed to let the heavy window down and went back to bed, wet, but confident that I would not again be caught napping under such circumstances.

I had not been asleep many moments until I heard a voice call: "Miss, will you have your tea now?" I opened my eyes and saw a steward standing at the door awaiting a reply. I refused the tea, as did the English girl on the other side of my cabin, managing to answer her bright smile with a very tired one, and then I was off to sleep again.

"Miss, will you have your bath now?" a voice broke in on my slumbers shortly afterwards. I looked up in disgust at a little white-capped woman who was bending over me, tempted to say I had just had my bath, a shower-bath, but thought better of it before speaking. I know I said something about "in a few minutes," and then I was asleep again.

"Well, you are a lazy girl! You'll miss your bath and breakfast if you don't get up the instant," was my third greeting. My surprise at the familiarity of the remark got the better of my sleepiness, and I thought:

"Well, by all that is wonderful, where am I? Am I in school again that a woman dare assume such a tone to me?" I kept my thoughts to myself, and said stiffly:

"I generally get up when I feel so inclined."

I saw my room-mate was missing, but I felt like sleeping and I decided to sleep; whether it pleased the stewardess or not, it mattered little to me. The steward was the next one to put in an appearance.

"Miss, this ship is inspected every day and I must have this cabin made up before they come," he said complainingly. "The captain will be here presently."

There was nothing to do but to get up, which I did. I found my way to the bath-room, but soon saw that it was impossible for me to turn on the water, as I did not understand the mechanism of the faucet. I asked a steward I saw outside the door, the whereabouts of the stewardess, and was simply amazed to hear him reply:

"The stewardess is taking a rest and cannot be disturbed."

After dressing I wandered up on the next deck and was told that breakfast was over long ago. I went out on deck, and the very first glimpse of the lazy looking passengers in their summer garments, lounging about in comfortable positions, or slowly promenading the deck, which was sheltered from the heat of the sun by a long stretch of awnings, and the smooth, velvety looking water, the bluest I had ever seen, softly gurgling against the side of the ship as it almost imperceptibly steamed on its course, and the balmy air, soft as a rose leaf, and just as sweet, air such as one dreams about but seldom finds; standing there alone among strange people, on strange waters, I thought how sweet life is!

Before an hour had passed I was acquainted with several persons. I had thought and expected that the English passengers would hold themselves aloof from a girl who was traveling alone, but my cabin-companion saw me before I got away from the door, and came forward to ask me to join herself and friends. We first had an amusing search for the steamer-chair which I had told the guard to buy at Brindisi and send on before our departure. There were over three hundred passengers on the ship, and I suppose they averaged a chair apiece, so it can easily be pictured the trouble it would be to find a chair among that number. I asked where the deck-stewards were when at last I felt the search was useless, and was surprised to learn that a deck-steward was an unknown commodity on the P. and O. line.

"I presume the quarter-master has charge of the decks," my companion said in conclusion, "but we are expected to look after our own chairs and rugs, and if we don't it is useless to inquire for them if they disappear."

Shortly before noon I became acquainted with an Englishman who belongs to the Civil Service in Calcutta. He had been in India for the last twenty years, during which time he had repeatedly visited England, which made this trip an old story to him. He had made the same trip from Calais on the India express as I had, and said he noticed me on the train. Learning that I was traveling alone, he devoted most of his time looking out for my comfort and pleasure.

The bugle blew for luncheon, which is always called by the Indian title "tiffin" on ships traveling in Eastern seas. The Englishman asked if I would go with him to tiffin, and as I had gone without breakfast I was only too anxious to go at the first opportunity. The dining-hall is on the second deck. It is a small room nicely decorated with tropical foliage plants and looks quite cozy and pretty, but it was never intended to accommodate a ship carrying more than seven-five first-class passengers.

The head-waiter, who stood at the door, stared at us blankly as we went in. I hesitated, naturally thinking that he would show us to some table, but as he did not I suggested to the gentleman with me, that he ask before we take our places.

"Sit anywhere," was the polite reply we received, so we sat down at the table nearest.

We had just been served, when four women ranging from twenty-four to thirty-five came in, and with indignant snorts of surprise, seated themselves at the same table. They were followed by a short, fat woman with a sweeping walk and air of satisfied assurance, who eyed us in a supercilious way and then turned to the others with an air of injured dignity that was intensely amusing. They were followed by two men and as there were only places for seven at the table the elderly man went out. Two of the girls sat on a lounge at the end of the table, which made room for the young man. Then we were made to suffer. All kinds of rude remarks were made about us. "They did hate people coming to their table;" "Too bad papa was robbed of his place;" "Shame people had to be crowded from their own table," and similar pleasant speeches were hurled at us. The young woman who sat at my left was not content to confine her rudeness to her tongue, but repeatedly reached across my plate, brushing my food with her sleeves without one word of apology. I confess I never had a more disagreeable meal. I thought at first that this rudeness was due to my being an American and that they had taken this means of showing their hatred for all Americans. Still I could not understand why they should subject an Englishman to the same treatment unless it was because he was with me. After-experiences showed me that my first conclusion was wrong; that I was not insulted because I was an American, but because the people were simply ill-bred. When dinner came we found that we were debarred from the dining-room. Passengers who got on at London were given the preference, and as there was not accommodations for all, the passengers who boarded the ship at Brindisi had to wait for second dinner.

One never realizes, until they face such contingencies, what an important part dinner plays in one's life. It was nine o'clock when the dining-room was cleared that night, and the Brindisi passengers were allowed to take their places at the table. I hardly believe they took much else. Everything was brought to us as it was left from the first dinner—cold soup, the remnants of fish, cut up bits of beef and fowl—all down the miserable course until at last came cold coffee! I had thought the food on the India Express might have been better until after my experience on the P. & O. steamer Victoria, and then I decided it might have been worse.

Such a roar of complaint as went up from those late dinner passengers. They wanted to get up a protest to serve on the captain, but I refused to take any part in it, and several of the more conservative ones followed my example.

The two women I have already referred to as having traveled on the India Express to Brindisi, were treated even worse than I was. When we made inquiries, we were told that at dinner only were the places reserved, but that at breakfast and tiffin, first there were first served. Acting on this information they went in to early tiffin the following day, and a young man who sat at the head of an empty table said to them as they went to sit down:

"You can't sit there. I've reserved those places for some of my friends." They went to another table and after sitting down, were requested by some late comers to get up and give the places to them. The one woman cried bitterly over it.

"I am a grandmother, and this is the sixth trip I have made to Australia, and I was never treated so insultingly in my life."

There are circumstances under which a trip on the Mediterranean would be like a dream of Paradise. If one were in love, for instance; for they do say that people in love do not eat, and aside from the food, the trip is perfect. Probably it is a hope of finding the cure that will help them to forget a stomach void, that makes love the principal subject on the P. & O. boats. Travelers who care to be treated with courtesy, and furnished with palatable food, will never by any chance travel on the Victoria.

It is all rule and no practice on that ship. The impudence and rudeness of the servants in America is a standing joke, but if the servants on the Victoria are a sample of English servants, I am thankful to keep those we have, such as they are. I asked the stewardess to assist a woman who looked as if she was dying of consumption, to the deck with her rugs, only to be told in reply, that she would not help any one unless they came and requested her to do so.

I heard her tell a passenger one day, that she did not believe it was sickness, but laziness that ailed the woman. If complaints were made about the conduct of the servants, they were always met by the assertion that the servants had been for a long time in the company's employ, and would take privileges.

The commander of the ship set an example for rudeness. A Spanish gentleman of high position who was traveling to China, where he represented his country in the diplomatic service, also got on at Brindisi. He thought that his first duty was to pay his respects to the Captain in charge of the ship, so he asked some one to point the Captain out to him. This was done on deck. He walked up to the Captain, and with a profound bow, hat in hand, begged the Captain's pardon, and said that he was *chargé d'affaires* of China and Siam for the Spanish government, and he wished to pay his duty and respects to the Captain of the boat on which he was traveling. The Captain glared at him savagely for a moment after he had finished, and then asked rudely:

"Well, what of it?"

The Spaniard was speechless for a moment, but recovering, he said politely:

"I beg your pardon, I thought I was addressing a gentleman and the commander of this ship." Turning, he walked away, and they never spoke afterwards.

Although I had brought a letter to the Captain, he never noticed me in any way. A bright faced, jolly boy, who was going to Hong Kong to enter a banking house of his uncle's, brought a letter to the Captain. He presented himself one day on deck, stepping a foot or so away until the Captain should have time to read it and greet him. The Captain read the letter, folded it carefully, put it in his pocket, and walked away! He never spoke to the boy afterwards, and the boy was careful not to give him that trouble. The Captain had a tongue for gossip, too. Every time I heard a slighting story about any of the passengers, and would ask where it came from, the answer would always be the Captain had told it to somebody.

Notwithstanding all annoying trifles it was a very happy life we spent in those pleasant waters. The decks were filled all the day, and when the lights were put out at night the passengers reluctantly went to their cabins. The passengers formed two striking contrasts. There were some of the most refined and lovely people on board, and there were some of the most ill-bred and uncouth. Most of the women, whose acquaintance I formed, were very desirous of knowing all about American women, and frequently expressed their admiration for the free American woman, many going so far as to envy me, while admiring my unfettered happiness. Two clever Scotch women I met were traveling around the world, but are taking two years at it. One Irishwoman, with a laugh that rivaled her face in sweetness, was traveling alone to Australia. My cabin-mate was bound for New Zealand, but she was accompanied by her brother, a pleasant young Englishman, who insisted on relinquishing his place at first dinner in my favor, and who stayed away despite my protests and my determination not to deprive him of a warm dinner.

In the daytime the men played cricket and quoits. Sometimes, in the evenings, we had singing, and other times we went to the second-class deck and listened to better music given by second-class passengers. When there were no chairs we would all sit down on the deck, and I remember nothing that was more enjoyable than these little visits. There was one little girl with a pale, slender face, who was a great favorite with us all, though none of us ever spoke to her. She sang in a sweet, pathetic voice a little melody about "Who'll buy my silver herrings?" until, I know, if she had tried to sell any, we should all have bought. The best we could do was to join her in the refrain, which we did most heartily.

Better than all to me, it was to sit in a dark corner on deck, above where the sailors had their food, and listen to the sounds of a tom-tom and a weird musical chanting that always accompanied their evening meal. The sailors were Lascars. They were not interesting to look at, and doubtless, if I could have seen as well as heard them at their evening meal, it would have lost its charm for me. They were the most untidy looking lot of sailors I ever saw. Over a pair of white muslin drawers they wore a long muslin slip very like in shape to the old-time night-shirt. This was tied about the waist with a colored handkerchief, and on their heads they wore gayly colored turbans, which are really nothing but a crown of straw with a scarf-shaped piece of bright cloth, often six feet in length, wound about the head. Their brown feet are always bare. They chant, as all sailors do, when hoisting sails, but otherwise are a grim, surly looking set, climbing about over the ship like a pack of monkeys.

When I boarded the boat at Brindisi the purser gave me some cables that had been sent to me, care of the Victoria. After we had been out several days, a young woman came to me with an unsealed cable and asked if I was Nellie Bly. Upon telling her I was, she said that the purser had given the cable to some of the passengers the day before, as he did not know who Nellie Bly was, and after two days traveling among them it reached me. Occasionally we would have a dance on deck to the worst music it has ever been my misfortune to hear. The members of the band also washed the dishes, and though I could not blame the passengers who always disappeared at the appearance of the musicians still I felt sorry for them; it was both ridiculous and pathetic that they should be required to cultivate two such inharmonious arts! One of the officers told me that the band they had before were compelled to scrub the decks, and their hands became so rough from the work that it was impossible for them longer to fill the role of musicians, so they were discharged and the new band were turned into dish-washers instead of deck-scrubbers.

I had not been on the Victoria many days until some one who had become friendly with me, told me it was rumored on board that I was an eccentric American heiress, traveling about with a hair brush and a bank book. I judged that some of the attention I was receiving was due to the story of my wealth. I found it convenient, later on, to correct the report when a young man came to me to say that I was the kind of a girl he liked, and as he was the second son and his brother would get both the money and the title, his sole ambition was to find a wife who would settle £1,000 a year on him.

There was another young man on board who was quite as unique a character and much more interesting to me. He told me that he had been traveling constantly since he was nine years old, and that he had always killed the desire to love and marry because he never expected to find a woman who could travel without a number of trunks, and bundles innumerable. I noticed that he dressed very exquisitely and changed his apparel at least three times a day, so my curiosity made me bold enough to ask how many trunks he carried with him.

"Nineteen," was the amazing reply. I no longer wondered at his fears of getting a wife who could not travel without trunks.

VII

"Two Beautiful Black Eyes"

I t was in the afternoon when the Victoria anchored at Port Said. We
were all on deck eagerly watching for the first sight of land, and
though that sight showed us a wide, sandy beach, and some uninteresting
two-storied white houses with arcade fronts, still it did not lessen our
desire to go ashore. I suppose that would have been the result under the
circumstances had Port Said been the most desolate place on earth. I
know everybody was experiencing a slight weariness, though we should
all have stoutly denied such a reflection on our constant companions,
and gladly welcomed the change of a few hours on shore, where at least
we might see new faces. A more urgent reason still, for our going to land,
was the fact that this was a coaling port for the Victoria, and I never
knew of anything that would make one more quickly feel that there are
things in life much worse than death, if I may use the expression, than
to have to stay on board a ship during the coaling operation.

Before the boat anchored the men armed themselves with canes, to
keep off the beggars they said; and the women carried parasols for the
same purpose. I had neither stick nor umbrella with me, and refused all
offers to accept one for this occasion, having an idea, probably a wrong
one, that a stick beats more ugliness into a person than it ever beats out.

Hardly had the anchor dropped than the ship was surrounded with
a fleet of small boats, steered by half-clad Arabs, fighting, grabbing,
pulling, yelling in their mad haste to be first. I never in my life saw such
an exhibition of hungry greed for the few pence they expected to earn
by taking the passengers ashore. Some boatmen actually pulled others
out of their boats into the water in their frantic endeavors to steal each
other's places. When the ladder was lowered, numbers of them caught
it and clung to it as if it meant life or death to them, and here they clung
until the captain was compelled to order some sailors to beat the Arabs
off, which they did with long poles, before the passengers dared venture
forth. This dreadful exhibition made me feel that probably there was
some justification in arming one's self with a club.

Our party were about the first to go down the ladder to the boats.
It had been our desire and intention to go ashore together, but when

we stepped into the first boat some were caught by rival boatmen and literally dragged across to other boats. The men in the party used their sticks quite vigorously; all to no avail, and although I thought the conduct of the Arabs justified this harsh course of treatment, still I felt sorry to see it administered so freely and lavishly to those black, half-clad wretches, and marveled at their stubborn persistence even while cringing under the blows. Having our party divided there was nothing to do under the circumstances but to land and reunite on shore, so we ordered the Arabs to pull away. Midway between the Victoria and the shore the boatmen stopped and demanded their money in very plain and forcible English. We were completely at their mercy, as they would not land us either way until we paid what they asked. One of the Arabs told me that they had many years' experience in dealing with the English and their sticks, and had learned by bitter lessons that if they landed an Englishman before he paid they would receive a stinging blow for their labor.

Walking up the beach, sinking ankle deep in the sand at every step, we came to the main street. Almost instantly we were surrounded by Arab boys who besought us to take a ride on the burros that stood patiently beside them. There were burros of all colors, sizes and shapes, and the boys would cry out, most beseechingly, "Here's Gladstone! Take a ride; see Gladstone with two beautiful black eyes."

This they would cry in such a soft plaintive way that one felt the "two beautiful black eyes" made the animals irresistible.

If one happened to be of a different political belief and objected to riding the Gladstone hobby, as it were, a choice could be made of almost any well-known, if not popular name. There were Mrs. Maybricks, Mary Andersons, Lillie Langtrys, and all the prominent men of the time.

I knew all about burros, having lived for some time in Mexico, but they proved to be quite a novelty to many of the passengers, almost all of whom were anxious to take a ride before returning to the boat. So, as many as could find animals to ride, mounted and went flying through that quaint, sleeping town, yelling with laughter, bouncing like rubber balls on their saddles, while half-naked Arab boys goaded the burros on by short, urgent hisses, and by prodding them from behind with a sharp stick.

After seeing about fifty of our passengers started off in this happy manner, a smaller number of us went to a gambling house, and in a short time were deep in the sport of placing our English gold on colors and numbers and waiting anxiously for the wheel to go 'round to see the money at last swept in by the man at the table. I do not think that any one of us knew anything about the game, but we recklessly put our money on the table and laughed to see it taken in by the man who gave the turn to the wheel.

There was another attraction in this place which helped to win a number of young men from that very expensive table. It was an orchestra composed of young women, some of whom were quite pleasing both in looks and manners.

The longer we remained at this gambling house the less money we had to spend in the shops. I went ashore with the determination not to buy anything as I was very anxious not to increase my baggage. I withstood the tempting laces which were offered at wonderfully low prices, the quaint Egyptian curios, and managed to content myself by buying a sun hat, as everybody else did; and a pugaree to wind about it, as is customary in the East.

Having bought a hat and seen all I cared to of the shops I went strolling about with some friends feasting my eyes on what were to me peculiarities of a peculiar people. I saw old houses with carved-wood fronts that would have been worth a fortune in America occupied by tenants that were unmistakably poor. The natives were apparently so accustomed to strangers that we attracted very little, if any attention, except from those who hoped to gain something from our visit. Unmolested we went about finding no occasion to use sticks on the natives. We saw a great number of beggars who, true to their trade, whined forth, with outstretched hands, their plaintive appeals, but they were not so intrusive or bothersome that they necessitated our giving them the cane instead of alms. The majority of these beggars presented such repulsive forms of misery that in place of appealing to my sympathetic nature, as is generally the case, they had a hardening effect on me. They seemed to thrust their deformities in our faces in order to compel us to give money to buy their absence from our sight.

While standing looking after a train of camels that had just come in loaded with firewood I saw some Egyptian women. They were small in stature and shapelessly clad in black. Over their faces, beginning just below the eyes, they wore black veils that fell almost to their knees. As if fearing that the veil alone would not destroy all semblance of features they wear a thing that spans the face between the hair and the veil down the line of their noses. In some cases this appears to be of gold, and in others it is composed of some black material. One Egyptian woman carried a little naked baby with her. She held it on her hips, its little black legs clinging to her waist much after the fashion of a boy climbing a pole.

Down at the beach we came upon a group of naked men clustered about an alligator that they had caught. It was securely fastened in some knotted rope, the end of which was held by some half dozen black fellows. The public water-carriers, with well filled goat-skins flung across their backs, we met making their way to the town for the last trip that day.

Darkness came on us very suddenly and sent us rushing off for our ship. This time we found the boatman would not permit us even to enter their boats until we paid them to take us across to the Victoria. Their price now was just double what they had charged to bring us to land. We protested, but they said it was the law to double the price after sunset.

They were just finishing the coaling when we reached the ship, but the sight we caught of the coal barges, lighted by some sputtering, dripping stuff, held in iron cages on the end of long poles, that showed the hurrying naked people rushing with sacks of coal up a steep gangplank, between the barges and the ship, was one long to be remembered. Nor were they working quietly. Judging from the noise, every one of them was yelling something that pleased his own fancy and humor.

The next morning I got up earlier than usual so anxious was I to see the famous Suez Canal. Rushing up on deck, I saw we were passing through what looked like an enormous ditch, enclosed on either side with high sand banks. We seemed to be hardly moving, which made us feel the heat very intensely. They tell me, that according to law, a ship must not travel through the canal at a speed exceeding five knots an hour, because a rapid passage of the ship would make a strong current that would wash in the sand banks. One gentleman, who had traveled all his life, helped us to pass some of the tedious, stifling hours in the canal by telling us the history of it.

It was begun in 1859 and took ten years to build. The work is estimated to have cost nearly £18,250,000, although the poor blacks that were employed to do the labor commanded the lowest possible wages. It is claimed that the lives of 100,000 laborers were sacrificed in the building of this canal, which is only 100 English miles, 88 geographical miles, 5 in length.

When first completed the width of the surface of the canal was three hundred and twenty-five feet, but the constant washing in of the banks has reduced it to one hundred and ninety-five feet. The bottom is said to be seventy-two feet wide and the depth is but twenty-six feet. The trip through the canal can be made in from twenty to twenty-four hours.

About noon of our first day in the canal we anchored in the bay fronting Ismailia. Here passengers were taken on, which gave us time to see the Khedive's palace, which is built a little way back from the beach in the heart of a beautiful green forest. Continuing the journey through the canal we saw little of interest. The signal stations were the only green spots that met the eye, but they were proof of what could be done, even in this sandy desert by the expenditure of time and energy.

The one thing that enlivened this trip was the appearance of naked Arabs, who would occasionally run along the banks of the canal, crying in pitiful tones, "bahkshish." This we understood meant money, which many of the kind hearted passengers would throw to them, but the beggars never seemed to find it, and would keep on after us, still crying, "bahkshish" until they were exhausted.

We passed several ships in the canal. Generally the passengers would call to the passengers on the other ships, but the conversation was confined mainly to inquiries as to what kind of a voyage had been theirs. We saw at one place in the canal, a lot of Arabs, both men and women, at work. Among them were a number of camels that were employed in carrying stone with which the laborers were endeavoring to strengthen the banks.

In the night the boat hung an electric light from the front, and by the aid of this light, moving it from side to side, were able to continue on their way. Before the introduction of electric head lights for this purpose, the vessels were always compelled to tie up in the canal over night, because of the great danger of running into the sand banks. In addition to making the trip longer, this stoppage added greatly to the discomfort of the passengers, who found that even the slow motion of the boat, helped, in a measure, to lessen the stifling heat that seemed to come from out the sand banks during the night as well as when the blazing sun was in the cloudless sky.

We saw, when near the end of the canal, several Arab encampments. They were both picturesque and interesting. First we would notice a small dull red fire, and between that fire and us we could see the outlines of people and resting camels. At one encampment we heard music, but at the others we saw the people either working over the fire, as if preparing their evening meal, or in sitting positions crouching about it in company with their camels.

Shortly after this we dropped anchor in the Bay of Suez. Hardly had we done so when the ship was surrounded by a number of small sail boats that, in the semi-darkness, with their white sails before the breeze, reminded me of moths flocking to a light, both from their white, winged-like appearance, and the rapid way in which numbers of them floated down on us. These sail boats were filled with men with native fruits, photographs and odd shells to sell. They all came on board, and among them were a number of jugglers. The passengers took very little interest in the venders, but all had a desire to see what was to be offered by the jugglers. There was one among them, a black man, who wore little else than a sash, a turban and a baggy pocket, in the lining of which he carried two lizards and a small rabbit. He was very anxious to show us his tricks and to get the money for them. He refused, however, to do anything with the rabbit and lizards until after he had shown us what he could do with a handkerchief and some bangles that he brought along for this purpose. He selected me from among the crowd, to hold the handkerchief, which he had first shaken as if to show us that it contained nothing. He then showed us a small brass bangle, and pretended to put the bangle in the handkerchief; he then placed the handkerchief in my hand, telling me to hold it tightly. I did so, feeling the presence of the bangle very plainly. He blew on it and jerking the handkerchief loose from my grasp, shook it. Much to the amazement of the crowd the bangle was gone. Some of the passengers in the mean time stole the juggler's rabbit, and one of the lizards had quietly taken itself off to some secluded spot. He was very much concerned about the loss of them and refused to perform any more tricks until they were restored to his keeping. At last one young man took the rabbit from his pocket and returned it to the juggler, much to his gratification. The lizard was not to be found, and as it was time for the ship to sail, the juggler was forced to return to his boat. After he had gone, several people came to know if I had any idea how the trick with the handkerchief had been done. I explained to them that it was an old and very uninteresting trick; that the man had one bangle sewn in the handkerchief, and the other bangle, which he showed to the people, he slipped quietly out of sight. Of course, the one who held the handkerchief held the bangle, but when the juggler would jerk the handkerchief from the hand, and shake it, in full view of his audience, the bangle being sewn to the handkerchief, would naturally not fall to the floor, and as he carefully kept the side to which the bangle was attached turned towards himself, he successfully duped his audience into thinking, that by his magic, he had made the bangle disappear. One of the men who listened to this explanation became very indignant, and wanted to know if I knew positively how this trick had been done, and why I had not exposed the man. I merely explained that I wanted to see the juggler get his money, much to the disgust of the Englishman.

Where we anchored at Suez some claim is the historic place where the Israelites crossed the Red Sea. Some people who bother themselves greatly about facts, figures and ancient history, bought views, which showed that at certain stages of the tide, people, in even this day, can wade around there without any risk of life or comfort. The next morning when we arose we were out of sight of land and well out on the Red Sea. The weather now was very hot, but still some of the passengers did their best to make things lively on board. One evening a number of young men gave a minstrel show. They displayed both energy and perseverance in preparing for it as well as in the execution of it. One end of the deck was set aside for the show. A stage was put up and the whole corner was enclosed by awnings, and the customary green curtain hung in place during service, as drop curtain between acts, as well appearing before and after the performance.

The young men filled their different roles in a very commendable manner, but as the night was so dreadfully warm, the passengers feeling the heat more than usual, owing to the deck being enclosed by awnings, it was difficult to awake any enthusiasm on the part of the audience. We had an intermission, when all retired to the dining room for punch and biscuits, and I know that no one appreciated the refreshments more than the actors, who joined us, their blackened faces streaked with perspiration.

Towards the last the passengers could find very little to do that proved interesting or in any way aided them to forget the heat. A few of those who could sing, or imagined they could, were persuaded to exercise their vocal organs for the benefit of those who could sing and would not, and those who realized they had no voice and knew enough to remain quiet. At other times many of us went to the deck reserved for the second-class passengers and enjoyed the concerts given by them. When there were no chairs for us on this deck we would sit on the floor, and we all acknowledged that the first-class passengers could not furnish music that was any better.

The days were spent mainly on deck lounging about in easy chairs. I found that no one enjoyed as much comfort as I did. I had changed my heavy waist for my silk bodice, and I felt cool and comfortable and lazily happy. When dinner hour approached we would see a few rush off to dress for dinner and later they would appear in full dress, low bodice and long train, much to the amusement of that class of passengers who maintained that it was decidedly not the thing to appear in full dress on an ocean steamer.

The evening dress, made of white linen, in which the young men in the East generally made their appearance at dinner, impressed me as being not only comfortable and appropriate, but decidedly becoming and elegant.

It is very seldom that men do not get more enjoyment out of life than women under like circumstances. Between cricket, to which they were passionately attached, and quoits and the smoking-room, which was the scene of many exciting games for large stakes and, later on, an hour or so spent in a dark corner of the deck pleasing and being pleased by some congenial companion of the opposite sex, the enforced rest was quite an agreeable one to the men.

We were all very much interested and concerned about a small bird that had traveled with us from Suez, sometimes flying along a little way and then resting on the rigging of the ship. It was a pretty bird with a slender gray tail and a silver breast and a black ring about its throat, its back being a modest drabish brown. At first it was easily frightened but after awhile it became very tame and would light on the deck among the passengers, picking up the crumbs they threw to it. Beside the bird as a topic of interest we had the lizard which was left behind by the juggler.

It was found in a quiet corner of the deck by the quarter-master the morning following our stop at Suez. A sympathizing young man took charge of it and endeavored to feed it, but after living in sullen quietness for a few days, it ceased to breathe and its death was solemnly announced to the passengers.

The Victoria is said to be the finest boat on the P. and O. Line, still it could not be more unsuited for the trip. It is very badly planned, being built so that a great number of cabins inside are absolutely cut off from light and air. It is a compliment to call them cabins as they are really nothing more than small, dark, disagreeable, and unventilated boxes. The passengers are charged all the same rate of fare, and if they are consigned to one of these undesirable boxes there is no redress; they must simply bow before the dictates of this company, who trade on the fact of their being an old established line, and a very desirable one in many respects, and passengers are treated—I judge only by what I saw and heard—as if they should consider that a favor had been conferred upon them when they were permitted to pay for tickets to travel on that line. The prices to ports that are touched at by rival steamship lines are rather reasonable, while to ports where they have the monopoly they charge exorbitant rates. I have stated that the conduct of the officers and servants, and the quality of the food left much to be desired by travelers.

The nights were so warm while on the Red Sea that the men left their cabins and spent their nights on deck. It is usually customary for the women to sleep on deck, one side of which, at such times, is reserved exclusively for them. During this trip none of the women had the courage to set the example, so the men had the decks to themselves.

Sleeping down below was all the more reason why women arising early would go on the decks before the sun began to boil in search of a refreshing spot where they could get a breath of cool air. At this hour the men were usually to be seen promenading about in their pajamas, but I heard no objections raised until much to the dismay of the women the Captain announced that the decks belonged to the men until after eight o'clock in the morning, and that the women were expected to remain below until after that hour.

Just before we came to Aden we passed in the sea a number of high brown mountains. They are known as the Twelve Apostles. Shortly after this we came in sight of Aden. It looked to us like a large, bare mountain of wonderful height, but even by the aid of glasses we were unable to tell that it was inhabited. Shortly after eleven o'clock in the morning we anchored in the bay. Our boat was soon surrounded by a number of small boats, which brought to us men who had things to sell, and the wonderful divers of the East.

The passengers had been warned by the officers on board not to go ashore at Aden because of the intense heat. So the women spent their time bargaining with the Jews who came to the ship to sell ostrich feathers and feather boas. The men helped them to close with the sellers always to the sellers' advantage, much as they might congratulate themselves to the contrary.

I, in company with a few of the more reckless ones, decided to brave the heat and go ashore and see what Aden had to offer.

VIII

ADEN TO COLOMBO

Hiring a large boat, I went ashore with a half dozen acquaintances who felt they could risk the sun. The four oarsmen were black fellows, thin of limb, but possessed of much strength and tireless good humor. They have, as have all the inhabitants of Aden, the finest white teeth of any mortals. This may be due to the care they take of them and the manner of that care. From some place, I am unable to state where, as I failed to see one living thing growing at Aden, they get tree branches of a soft, fibrous wood which they cut into pieces three and four inches in length. With one end of this stick, scraped free of the bark, they rub and polish their teeth until they are perfect in their whiteness. The wood wears into a soft pulp, but as one can buy a dozen sticks for a penny one can well afford to throw the stick away after once using; although, if necessary, a stick can be used many times. I bought several sticks and found them the most efficient as well as pleasant tooth brush I had ever tried. I felt a regret that some enterprising firm had not thought of importing this useful bit of timber to replace the tooth-destroying brush used in America.

The man in charge of the boat that carried us to land was a small black fellow with the thinnest legs I ever saw. Somehow they reminded me of smoked herrings, they were so black, flat and dried looking. He was very gay notwithstanding his lack of weight. Around his neck and over his bare breast were twined strings of beads, black and gold and silver. Around his waist was a highly colored sash, and on his arms and ankles were heavy bracelets, while his fingers and toes seemed to be trying to outdo one another in the way of rings. He spoke English quite well, and to my rather impertinent question as to what number constituted his family told me that he had three wives and eleven children, which number, he added piously, by the grace of the power of his faith, he hoped to increase.

His hair was yellow which, added to his very light dress of jewelry and sash, gave him rather a strange look. The bright yellow hair and the black skin forming a contrast which was more startling than the black eyes and yellow hair that flashed upon the astonished vision of the American public some years ago, but has become since an old and tiresome sight. Some of the boatmen had their black wool pasted down and hidden under a coating of lime. I was very curious about it until the first man explained that they were merely bleaching their hair; that it was always done by covering the head with lime, which, being allowed to remain on for several days, exposed to the hot sun and the water, bleached the hair yellow or red at the expiration of that time. This bleaching craze, he also informed me, was confined to the men of Aden. So far, none of the women had tried to enhance their black beauty in that way, but it was considered very smart among the men.

While we were talking our men were vigorously pulling to the time of a rousing song, one line of which was sung by one man, the others joining in the refrain at the end. Their voices were not unpleasant, and the air had a monotonous rhythm that was very fascinating.

We landed at a well-built pier and walked up the finely-cut, white-stone steps from the boat to the land. Instantly we were surrounded by half-clad black people, all of whom, after the manner of hack-drivers at railway stations, were clamoring for our favor. They were not all drivers, however. Mingling with the drivers were merchants with jewelry, ostrich plumes and boas to sell, runners for hotels, beggars, cripples and guides. This conglomeration besought us to listen to every individual one of them until a native policeman, in the Queen's uniform, came forward and pushed the black fellows back with his hands, sometimes hastening their retreat with his boot.

A large board occupied a prominent position on the pier. On it was marked the prices that should be paid drivers, boatmen, and like people. It was, indeed, a praiseworthy thoughtfulness that caused the erection of that board, for it prevented tourists being robbed. I looked at it, and thought that even in that land there was more precaution taken to protect helpless and ignorant strangers than in New York city, where the usual custom of night hack-men is to demand exorbitant prices, and if they are not forthcoming, to pull off their coats and fight for it.

Perched on the side of this bleak, bare mountain is a majestic white building, reached by a fine road cut in the stone that forms the mountain. It is a club house, erected for the benefit of the English soldiers who are stationed on this barren spot. In the harbor lay an English man-of-war, and near a point where the land was most level, numbers of white tents were pitched for soldiers.

From the highest peak of the black, rocky mountain, probably

1700 feet above sea level, floated the English flag. As I traveled on and realized more than ever before how the English have stolen almost all, if not all, desirable sea-ports, I felt an increased respect for the level-headedness of the English government, and I cease to marvel at the pride with which Englishmen view their flag floating in so many different climes and over so many different nationalities.

Near the pier were shops run by Parsees. A hotel, post-office and telegraph office are located in the same place. The town of Aden is five miles distant. We hired a carriage and started at a good pace, on a wide, smooth road that took us along the beach for a way, passing low rows of houses, where we saw many miserable, dirty-looking natives; passed a large graveyard, liberally filled, which looked like the rest of that stony point, bleak, black and bare, the graves often being shaped by cobblestones.

The roads at Aden are a marvel of beauty. They are wide and as smooth as hardwood, and as they twist and wind in pleasing curves up the mountain, they are made secure by a high, smooth wall against mishap. Otherwise their steepness might result in giving tourists a serious roll down a rough mountain-side.

Just before we began to ascend we saw a black man at his devotions. He was kneeling in the centre of a little square formed by rocks. His face was turned heavenward, and he was oblivious to all else except the power before which he was laying bare his inmost soul, with a fervor and devotion that commanded respect, even from those who thought of him as a heathen. I inferred that he was a sun worshipper from the way in which he constantly had his face turned upward, except when he bent forward to kiss the ground on which he knelt.

On the road we saw black people of many different tribes. A number of women I noticed, who walked proudly along, their brown, bare feet stepping lightly on the smooth road. They had long purple-black hair, which was always adorned with a long, stiff feather, dyed of brilliant red, green, purple, and like striking shades. They wore no other ornament than the colored feather, which lent them an air of pride, when seen beside the much-bejeweled people of that quaint town. Many of the women, who seemed very poor indeed, were lavishly dressed in jewelry. They did not wear much else, it is true, but in a place as hot as Aden, jewelry must be as much as anyone would care to wear.

To me the sight of these perfect, bronze-like women, with a graceful drapery of thin silk wound about the waist, falling to the knees, and a corner taken up the back and brought across the bust, was most bewitching. On their bare, perfectly modeled arms were heavy bracelets, around the wrist and muscle, most times joined by chains. Bracelets were also worn about the ankles, and their fingers and toes were laden with rings. Sometimes large rings were suspended from the nose, and the ears were almost always outlined with hoop rings, that reached from the inmost edge of the lobe to the top of the ear joining the head. So closely were these rings placed that, at a distance, the ear had the appearance of being rimmed in gold. A more pleasing style of nose ornament was a large gold ornament set in the nostril and fastened there as screw rings fasten in the ear. Still, if that nose ornamentation was more pleasing than the other, the ear adornment that accompanied it was disgusting. The lobe of the ear was split from the ear, and pulled down to such length that it usually rested on the shoulder. The enormous loop of flesh was partially filled with large gold knobs.

At the top of the hill we came to a beautiful, majestic, stone double gate, the entrance to the English fort and also spanning the road that leads to the town. Sentinels were pacing to and fro but we drove past them without stopping or being stopped, through a strange, narrow cut in the mountain, that towered at the sides a hundred feet above the road bed. Both these narrow, perpendicular sides are strongly fortified. It needs but one glance at Aden, which is in itself a natural fort, to strengthen the assertion that Aden is the strongest gate to India.

The moment we emerged from the cut, which, besides being so narrow that two carriages pass with great difficulty, is made on a dangerous steep grade, we got a view of the white town of Aden, nestling in the very heart of what seems to be an extinct volcano. We were driven rapidly down the road, catching glimpses of gaudily attired mounted policemen, water-carriers from the bay, with their well-filled goat-skins flung across their backs, camels loaded with cut stone, and black people of every description.

When we drove into the town, which is composed of low adobe houses, our carriage was surrounded with beggars. We got out and walked through an unpaved street, looking at the dirty, uninviting shops and the dirty, uninviting people in and about them. Very often we were urged to buy, but more frequently the natives stared at us with quiet curiosity. In the heart of the town we found the camel market, but beyond a number of camels standing, lying, and kneeling about, the sight was nothing extraordinary. Near by was a goat market, but business seemed dull in both places.

Without buying anything we started to return to the ship. Little naked children ran after us for miles, touching their foreheads humbly and crying for money. They all knew enough English to be able to ask us for charity.

When we reached the pier, we found our driver had forgotten all the English he knew when we started out. He wanted one price for the carriage and we wanted to pay another. It resulted in our appealing to a native policeman, who took the right change from us, handed it to the driver, and gave him, in addition, a lusty kick for his dishonesty.

Our limited time prevented our going to see the water tanks, which are some miles distant from Aden. When we returned to the ship we found Jews there, selling ostrich eggs and plumes, shells, fruit, spears of sword-fish, and such things. In the water, on one side of the boat, were numbers of men, Somali boys, they called them, who were giving an exhibition of wonderful diving and swimming.

They would actually sit in the water looking like bronze statues, as the sun rested on their wet, black skins. They sat in a row, and turning their faces up towards the deck, would yell methodically, one after the other, down the entire line:

"Oh! Yo! Ho!"

It sounded very like a chorus of bull-frogs and was very amusing. After finishing this strange music they would give us a duet, half crying, persuasively, in a sing-song style:

"Have a dive! Have a dive! Have a dive!"

The other half, meanwhile, would put their hands before their widely opened mouths, yelling through their rapidly moving fingers with such energy that we gladly threw over silver to see them dive and stop the din.

The moment the silver flashed over the water all the bronze figures would disappear like flying fish, and looking down we would see a few ripples on the surface of the blue water—nothing more. After a time that seemed dangerously long to us, they would bob up through the water again. We could see them coming before they finally appeared on the surface, and one among the number would have the silver between his teeth, which would be most liberally displayed in a broad smile of satisfaction. Some of these divers were children not more than eight years old, and they ranged from that up to any age. Many of them had their hair bleached. As they were completely naked, excepting a small cloth twisted about the loins, they found it necessary to make a purse out of their cheeks, which they did with as much ease as a cow stows away grass to chew at her leisure.

I have often envied a cow this splendid gift. One wastes so much time eating, especially when traveling, and I could not help picturing the comfort it would be sometimes to dispose of our food wholesale and consume it at our leisure afterwards. I am certain there would be fewer dyspeptics then.

No animal, waterborn and bred, could frisk, more gracefully in the water than do these Somali boys. They swim about, using the legs alone, or the arms alone, on their backs, or sides, and, in most cases, with their faces under water. They never get out of the way of a boat. They merely sink and come up in the same spot when the boat passes. The bay at Aden is filled with sharks, but they never touch these black men, so they tell me, and the safety with which they spend their lives in the water proves the truth of the assertion. They claim that a shark will not attack a black man, and after I had caught the odor of the grease with which these men annoint their bodies, I did not blame the sharks.

After a seven hours stay at Aden we left for Colombo, being followed a long ways out from land by the divers. One little boy went out with us on the ship, and when he left us he merely took a plunge from the upper deck into the sea and went happily back towards Aden, on his side, waving a farewell to us with his free hand.

The passengers endeavored to make the time pass pleasantly between Aden and Colombo. The young women had some *tableaux vivants* one evening, and they were really very fine. In one they wished to represent the different countries. They asked me to represent America, but I refused, and then they asked me to tell them what the American flag looked like! They wanted to represent one as nearly as possible and to rise it to drape the young woman who was to represent America. Another evening we had a lantern slide exhibition that was very enjoyable.

The loyalty of the English to their Queen on all occasions, and at all times, had won my admiration. Though born and bred a staunch American, with the belief that a man is what he makes of himself, not what he was born, still I could not help admiring the undying respect the English have for their royal family. During the lantern slide exhibition, the Queen's picture was thrown on the white sheet, and evoked warmer applause than anything else that evening. We never had an evening's amusement that did not end by everybody rising to their feet and singing "God Save the Queen." I could not help but think how devoted that woman, for she is only a woman after all, should be to the interests of such faithful subjects.

With that thought came to me a shamed feeling that there I was, a free born American girl, the native of the grandest country on earth, forced to be silent because I could not in honesty speak proudly of the rulers of my land, unless I went back to those two kings of manhood, George Washington and Abraham Lincoln.

IX

Delayed Five Days

About nine o'clock in the morning we anchored in the bay at Colombo, Ceylon. The island, with its abundance of green trees, was very restful and pleasing to our eyes after the spell of heat we had passed through on the ocean coming from Aden.

Preparations had been made by the passengers before we anchored, to go ashore, and as we came slowly into the small harbor, where a number of vessels were lying, we all stood impatiently on deck waiting for the first opportunity to desert the ship.

With all our impatience we could not fail to be impressed with the beauties of Colombo and the view from the deck of our incoming steamer. As we moved in among the beautiful ships laying at anchor, we could see the green island dotted with low arcaded buildings which looked, in the glare of the sun, like marble palaces. In the rear of us was the blue, blue sea, jumping up into little hills that formed into snow drifts which softly sank into the blue again. Forming the background to the town was a high mountain, which they told us was known as Adam's Peak. The beach, with a forest of tropical trees, looked as if it started in a point away out in the sea, curving around until near the harbor it formed into a blunt point, the line of which was carried out to sea by a magnificent breakwater surmounted by a light-house. Then the land curved back again to a point where stood a signal station, and on beyond a wide road ran along the water's edge until it was lost at the base of a high green eminence that stood well out over the sea, crowned with a castle-like building glistening in the sunlight.

Little boats filled with black-men, we could see coming out towards us from the shore, but my eyes were fastened on a strangely shaped object, resting on the surface of the water in the bay. It seemed a living, feathered thing of so strange a shape that I watched it with feelings akin to horror. What horrible feathered monster could that lovely island produce, I wondered, noticing with dismay that the ship was heading for it. Just as we were upon it, there was a flutter of wings and a cloud of birds flew across and settled down upon the breakwater, where some fishermen, their feet overhanging the stony sides, were watching their lines. I looked back at what had raised so much consternation in my mind, and saw now that it was relieved of a feathered mass off birds,—a harmless red buoy!

Accompanied by a friend, I was the first to step ashore. Some passengers who started in advance of us, took a steam launch. My escort said that he would give me a novel experience, and also show me a small boat that traveled faster than a steam launch. The gentleman who had offered to be my escort during our jaunt on land, was a traveler of vast experience. He has averaged a yearly tour of the world for several years, and knows the eastern countries as he knows his home. Still, when I saw the boat in which he intended to take me ashore, I rather doubted his judgment, but I said nothing.

The boat was a rudely constructed thing. The boat proper was probably five feet in length and two feet in width across the top, narrowing down to the keel, so that it was not wide enough to allow one's feet to rest side by side in the bottom. There were two seats in the middle of the boat facing one another. They are shaded by a bit of coffee sack that must be removed to give room for passengers to get in. The two men sit at either end of this peculiar boat, and with one paddle each. The paddle is a straight pole, with a board the shape and size of a cheese-box head tied to the end of it, and with both those paddles on the same side they row us ashore. The boat is balanced by a log the length of the boat and fastened out by two curved poles, probably three feet from the boat. These boats are called by tourists, outriggers, but are called by the people of Ceylon, catamarans.

With but slight exertion the men sent the boat cutting through the water, and in a few moments we had distanced the steam launch and had accommodations engaged at the hotel before the launch had landed its passengers. It is said at Colombo that catamarans are used by the native fisherman, who go out to sea in them, and that they are so seaworthy and so secure against capsizing that no case of an accident to a catamaran has ever been reported.

A nearer view of the hotel, the Grand Oriental, did not tend to lessen its attractiveness—in fact it increased it. It was a fine, large hotel, with tiled arcades, corridors airy and comfortable, furnished with easy chairs and small marble topped tables which stood close enough to the broad arm-rests, for one to sip the cooling lime squashes or the exquisite native tea, or eat of the delicious fruit while resting in an attitude of ease and laziness. I found no place away from America where smoking was prohibited, and in this lovely promenade the men smoked, consumed gallons of whiskey and soda and perused the newspapers, while the women read their novels or bargained with the pretty little copper-colored women who came to sell dainty hand-made lace, or with the clever, high-turbaned merchants who would snap open little velvet boxes and expose, to the admiring gaze of the charmed tourists, the most bewildering gems. There were deeply-dark emeralds, fire-lit diamonds, exquisite pearls, rubies like pure drops of blood, the lucky cat's-eye with its moving line, and all set in such beautiful shapes that even the men, who would begin by saying, "I have been sold before by some of your kind," would end by laying down their cigars and papers and examining the glittering ornaments that tempt all alike. No woman who lands at Colombo ever leaves until she adds several rings to her jewel box, and these rings are so well known that the moment a traveler sees one, no difference in what part of the globe, he says to the wearer, inquiringly:

"Been to Colombo, eh?"

For the first time since leaving America I saw American money. It is very popular in Colombo and commands a high price—as jewelry! It goes for nothing as money. When I offered it in payment for my bills I was told it would be taken at sixty per cent discount. The Colombo diamond merchants are very glad to get American twenty dollar gold pieces and pay a high premium on them. The only use they make of the money is to put a ring through it and hang it on their watch chains for ornaments. The wealth of the merchant can be estimated by his watch chain, they tell me; the richer the merchant the more American gold dangles from his chain. I saw some men with as many as twenty pieces on one chain. Most of the jewelry bought and sold in Colombo is sold in the corridor of the Grand Oriental Hotel. Merchants bring their wares with them and tourists find it pleasanter than visiting the shops.

Leading off from this corridor, pleasant in its coolness, interesting in its peculiarities, is the dining-hall, matching the other parts of the hotel with its picturesque stateliness. The small tables are daintily set and are richly decorated daily with the native flowers of Colombo, rich in color, exquisite in form, but void of perfume. From the ceiling were suspended embroidered punkas, that invention of the East which brings comfort during the hottest part of the day. The punkas are long strips of cloth, fastened to bamboo poles that are suspended within a short distance of the tables. They are kept in motion by a rope pulley, worked by a man or boy. They send a lazy, cooling air through the building, contributing much to the ease and comfort of the guest. Punkas are also used on all the ships that travel in the East.

Very good food was served at the hotel—which was all the more palatable to the passengers from the Victoria after the trials they had had for the past fortnight in eating the same kind of food under daily different names. Singalese waiters were employed, and they were not only an improvement on the English stewards, to whose carelessness and impudence we had been forced to submit, but they were interesting to the Westerner.

They managed to speak English very well and understood everything that was said to them. They are not unpleasing people, being small of stature and fine of feature, some of them having very attractive, clean-cut faces, light bronze in color. They wore white linen apron-like skirts and white jackets. Noiselessly they move over the smooth tile floor, in their bare, brown feet. Their straight black hair is worn long, twisted in a Psyche knot at the back of the head. On the crown of the head, instead of circling it from ear to ear, is always set a tortoise shell comb, like those worn by American school children. It was some time before I could tell a Singalese man from a Singalese woman. It is not difficult to distinguish the different sexes after one knows that the Singalese men wear the comb, which is as distinct a feature of their dress as men's trousers in America. Singalese women would not think of donning this little comb any more than a sensitive American woman would think of wearing men's apparel.

I did not hear the term waiter, or *garcon*, after leaving America. After leaving the English ships I did not hear the word steward, but instead, in the hotels and ships in the East, all the servants were called "boy." We can call "steward! . . . waiter! . . . garcon!" until we are weary, without any result, but the moment we whisper "boy!" a pleasant black fellow says, "yes, sir," at our side, and is ready to do our bidding.

At tiffin I had some real curry, the famous native dish of India. I had been unable to eat it on the Victoria, but those who knew said it was a most delicious dish when prepared rightly and so I tested it on shore. First a divided dish containing shrimps and boiled rice was placed before me. I put two spoonfuls of rice on my plate, and on it put one spoonful of shrimps; there was also chicken and beef for the meat part of the curry, but I took shrimps only. Then was handed me a much divided plate containing different preserved fruits, chuddah and other things hot with pepper. As instructed, I partook of three of this variety and put it on top of what had been placed first on my plate. Last came little dried pieces of stuff that we heard before we saw, its odor was so loud and unmistakable. They called it Bombay duck. It is nothing more or less than a small fish, which is split open, and after being thoroughly dried, is used with the curry. One can learn to eat it.

After all this is on the plate it is thoroughly mixed, making a mess very unsightly, but very palatable, as I found. I became so given to curry that I only stopped eating it when I found, after a hearty meal, curry threatened to give me palpitation of the heart. A story is told concerning the Bombay duck that is very amusing.

The Shah of Persia was notified that some high official in India intended to send him a lot of very fine Bombay duck. The Shah was very much pleased and, in anticipation of their arrival, had some expensive ponds built to put the Bombay ducks in! Imagine his consternation when he received those ill-smelling, dried fish!

After tiffin we drove to mount Lavania. We went along the smoothest, most perfectly made roads I ever saw. They seemed to be made of red asphalt, and I was afterwards told that they are constructed by convicts. Many of these roads were picturesque bowers, the over-reaching branches of the trees that lined the waysides forming an arch of foliage above our heads, giving us charming telescopic views of people and conveyances along the road. Thatched huts of the natives and glimpses of the dwellers divided our attention with the people we passed on the road.

Mount Lavania we found to be the place we had noticed on entering the harbor. It is a fine hotel situated on an eminence overlooking the sea, and is a favorite resort during the hot seasons. It is surrounded by a smooth green lawn and faces the blue sea, whence it gets a refreshing breeze all the year through.

After dinner, everybody at the Grand Oriental Hotel went out for a drive, the women, and many of the men going bare-headed. Driving through the town, down the wide streets, past beautiful homes set well back in tropical gardens, to the Galle Face drive that runs along the beach just out of reach of the waves that break on the sandy banks with a more musical roar than I ever heard water produce before. The road lies very close to the water's edge, and by the soft rays of the moon its red surface was turned to silver, the deep blue of the sea was black, and the foamy breakers were snow drifts. In the soft, pure light we would see silent couples strolling along arm and arm, apparently so near the breakers that I felt apprehensive lest one, stronger than the others, should catch them unawares and wash them out to that unknown land where we all travel to rest. Lounging on the benches that face the sea were occasional soldiers in the Queen's uniform, whom I looked at anxiously, unable to tell whether their attitude of weariness bespoke a rest from labor or hungry home-sickness. One night I saw a native standing waist deep fishing in the roaring breakers. They tell me that many of the fish bite more freely after night, but I thought how easily the fisherman might be washed away, and no one would be the wiser until his absence was noticed by his friends.

Where the Galle Face drive merges into another road, stands the Galle Face Hotel surrounded by a forest of palm trees. Lounging on long-bottomed, easy chairs, on the stone-floored and stone-pillared verandah, one can see through the forest of tall palms where the ocean kisses the sandy beach, and while listening to the music of the wave, the deep, mellow roar, can drift—drift out on dreams that bring what life has failed to give; soothing pictures of the imagination that blot out for a moment the stern disappointment of reality. Or, when the dreams fade away, one can drown the sigh with the cooling lime squash which the noiseless, bare-footed, living bronze has placed on the white arm-rest, at the same time lazily watching the jinrickshas come silently in through the gas-lit gate, the naked black runners coming to a sudden stop, letting the shafts drop so the passenger can step out.

Lazily I sat there one sweet, dusky night, only half hearing my escort's words that came to me mingled with the sound of the ocean. A couple stood close together, face bending over a face up-turned, hand clasped in hand and held closely against a manly heart, standing, two dark figures, beneath an arch of the verandah, outlined against the gate lamp. I felt a little sympathy for them as wrapped in that delusion that makes life heaven or hell, that forms the foundation for every novel, play or story, they stood, until a noisy new arrival wakened her from blissful oblivion, and she rushed, scarcely waiting for him to kiss the hand he held, away into the darkness. I sighed again, and taking another sip of my lime squash, turned to answer my companion.

Early next morning I was awakened by a Singalese waiter placing coffee and toast on a small table which he drew up close to my curtained bed, after which he went out. I knew from the dim light that crept in through the open glass door which led to the balcony, that it was still early, and I soon went off to sleep. I was awakened shortly by a rattling of the dishes on the table, and opening my eyes I saw, standing on the table, quietly enjoying my toast, a crow!

I was not then used to having toast and tea before arising, as is the custom in Ceylon, so I let the crow satisfy his appetite and leisurely take his departure without a protest. I arose earlier than was my habit, because I had a desire to see what there might be to see while I had the opportunity.

After a cool, refreshing bath, I dressed hastily and went down below. I found almost all of my friends up, some having already started out to enjoy the early morning. I regretted my generosity to the crow when I learned that breakfast was never served until nine o'clock, and as everybody endeavored to have the benefit of the cool, sweet morning, toast and tea was very sustaining.

In a light wagon we again drove down Galle Face road, and out past a lake in which men, women, children, oxen, horses, buffalo and dogs were sporting. It was a strange sight. Off on a little green island we saw the laundry folk at work, beating, sousing and wringing the clothes, which they afterwards spread upon the grass to dry. Almost all of the roads through which we drove were perfect with their picturesque curves, and often bordered and arched with magnificent trees, many of which were burdened with beautiful brilliant blossoms.

Everybody seemed to be out. The white people were driving, riding, riding bicycles, or walking. The breakwater, which is a good half mile in length, is a favorite promenade for the citizens of Colombo. Morning and evening gaily dressed people can be seen walking back and forth between the light-house and the shore. When the stormy season comes the sea dashes full forty feet above this promenade, which must be cleansed of a green slime, after the storms are over, before it can be traveled with safety. The Prince of Wales laid the first stone of this beautiful breakwater in 1875, and ten years later it was finished.

It is considered one of the finest in existence.

Colombo reminded me of Newport, R. I. Possibly—in my eyes, at least—Colombo is more beautiful. The homes may not be as expensive, but they are more artistic and picturesque. The roads are wide and perfect; the view of the sea is grand, and while unlike in its tropical aspect, still there is something about Colombo that recalls Newport.

After breakfast, which usually leaves nothing to be desired, guests rest in the corridor of the hotel; the men who have business matters to attend to look after them and return to the hotel not later than eleven. About the hour of noon everybody takes a rest, and after luncheon they take a nap. While they sleep the hottest part of the day passes, and at four they are again ready for a drive or a walk, from which they return after sunset in time to dress for dinner. After dinner there are pleasant little rides in jinrickshas or visits to the native theaters.

I went one night to a Parsee theatre. At the entrance were groups of people, some of whom were selling fruits, and some were jinricksha men waiting to haul the people home after the performance. There was no floor in the building. The chairs were placed in rows on the ground. the house was quite well filled with native men, women and children who were deeply interested in the performance which had begun before we reached there.

The actors were all men; my escort had told me women never think of going on the stage in that country. The stage was not unlike any other stage, and the scenery, painted by native artists, was quite as good as is usually seen. On the left of the stage, close to the wing, was a man, sitting cross-legged on a raised platform, beating a tom-tom. A tom-tom was undoubtedly the mother to the drum. It is made on the same principle, but instead of being round is inclined to be long in shape, The player uses his hands instead of drum-sticks, and when one becomes accustomed to it I do not think the sound of a tom-tom can be called unmusical. The musician who presided over the tom-tom this night was dressed in a thin white material, and he wore a very large turban of the same stuff on his head. His copper-colored face was long and earnest, and he beat the tom-tom with a will that was simply amazing when one was informed that he had been constantly engaged at it since nine in the morning. If his hands did not tire his legs did. Several times I saw him move, as if to find ease by shifting his squatting position, and every time I saw his bare feet turn up, in full view of the audience, I felt an irresistible desire to laugh.

On the right, directly opposite to the tom-tom player, was a man, whose duty it was to play a strange looking organ. He only used one hand, the left, for playing, and with the right he held a book, which he steadily perused throughout the entire performance, reading and playing mechanically without once looking at the actors.

The actors were amusing, at least. The story of the opera was not unlike those in other countries. The basis or plot of the play was a tale of love and tragedy. A tall young man, with his face painted a death-like white, sang shrilly through his very high-arched nose to another young man, dressed in the costume of a native woman. The latter was the lady, and the heroine of the play, and he sang sharply through his nose like his, or her, lover. All the actors sang through their noses, and the thinner their voices and the more nasal sound they employed the more the audience applauded.

The heroine of the play was a maid-servant employed by a very wealthy tea planter, who was the father of the lover who sang through his nose. The lover, like all lovers urged the girl to be his in songs that were issued through his nose for fifteen minutes at a time. He, the heroine, would endeavor to look shy all through this unsufferably long song of nasal sound, and then she would take up the same refrain, and to the same tune sing back at him for the same length, and after his own style, while he would hang his head and listen. Their gestures were very few, and they usually stood in one spot on the stage. Sometimes they would embrace, but only to fall apart and sing at each other again.

The play goes on. A bold, bad robber, whose chalk-whitened face has a most Jewish cast, sees the maid-servant and falls in love with her. She repels his advances and goes into her master's house. Then the robber puts a cross on the house and vows that he will return with his men to kill the inhabitants, for the heroine, in her simplicity, confesses to the truth of his supposition that she loves another, and that other is her master's son, so the villain swears that he will return, kill the people of the house, and not only carry off the wealth but the maidservant as well.

After the robber departs, the heroine comes out, and spies the cross upon her house. With a crafty look upon her face, she picks up the chalk which the robber had dropped, and marks all the other houses in the street in just the same way, so that when the robber returns he is foiled in his bold, bad game, for he cannot tell which house holds his charmer, and her wealthy lover and master. He is a patient robber, and lies in wait until the lovers come forth to coo on the street. While they are busy, making love through their noses, the man plays the organ with energy, the turbaned musician beats the tom-tom as if his life depended upon it, and the bold, bad robber clutches at his stomach, twists his face into the most agonized expressions, and otherwise shows his agony to the audience. When they go into the house he is about to follow, when the master appears, and, as he is going in, the robber approaches and, saying that he is a wealthy tea-merchant, begs to be permitted to rest at his house that night. The master most cordially consents, just as the heroine appears, and she, having heard the conversation tells her master not to allow the man to stay. The master becomes very angry at her boldness and promises her a liberal punishment, to take effect later in the day.

The merchant begs to be permitted to have his cases of tea placed within the garden-walls of his host, that the tea may be safe through the night. Of course the host consents, and the next scene shows the chests of tea in the garden, and the bold robber puts out the light at the door and goes into the house to bide his time. Even that heroine dreams, and, like other heroines, selects the cool, sweet night and the garden to dream in. She is surprised to find the garden in darkness, and lays her finger to the side of her nose when she sees the lamp is not burning. As she skips about, smelling the artificial flowers, the lid of a tea-chest is raised slightly, and a man sings something through his nose. She starts back in surprise, but instead of screaming, she answers the inquiry in nasal tones, and she learns that the chests are not filled with tea, but with men who belong to the robber, for whom they mistook her. When the man closes the lid again to wait the bidding to come forth, she deftly locks all the cases, and then calls upon a man servant who helps her, the heroine, to carry these cases containing men into a house in which they are securely locked.

The next scene shows a room in which the people are gathered and making merry. They are all sitting on the floor, and among them is the chief robber. The heroine, and other maidservants are brought in to give a dagger dance. They have bracelets of bells around their wrists and ankles, and the dance is very pleasing. The heroine and another servant dance while battling with each other with their knives. Occasionally they break apart and encircle the room, and the heroine makes motions as if she intended to give the guests a playful thrust. She sees the robber slyly poison her master's wine, and so she dances around the robber's way, and sticks her dagger in his heart and goes on with her dance. The guests laugh until they see the robber rise to his feet and fall dead. They see then the thrust was not playful but real, and the girl is caught and the master says she shall die. Then she screeches out the story of the men in the tea-cases and tells about the poisoned wine, and the guests applaud her brave act, and she is told to ask for any favor she wishes. She asks for her master's son! She gets him, to the music of the tom-tom and the organ, and I suppose they live happy ever afterwards.

I rode home from the theatre in a bullock hackery. It was a very small springless cart on two wheels with a front seat for the driver, and on the back seat, with our backs to the driver and out feet hanging over, we drove to the hotel. The bullock is a strange, modest-looking little animal with a hump on its back and crooked horns on its head. I feared that it could not carry us all, but it traveled at a very good pace. There was a sound of grunt, grunt, grunting that concerned me very much until l found it was the driver and not the bullock that was responsible for the noise. With grunts he urged the bullock to greater speed.

The drive, along tree-roofed roads, was very quiet and lovely. The moonlight fell beautiful and soft over the land, and nothing disturbed the stillness except the sound of the sea and an occasional soldier we met staggering along towards the barracks. At one place we saw a mosque with low, dim lamps hanging about. We went in and found the priests lying about on the stone floor, some at the very foot of the altar. We talked with them in whispers and then returned to the cart, which soon carried us back to the hotel. Just as we turned a corner to go to the hotel, an officer rushed up and, catching hold of a wheel, tried to stop the hackery, telling the driver that we were all under arrest.

The candles in one of the lamps had burned out and we were arrested for driving with a dark side. My companion made it right with the policeman, and we went to the hotel instead of the jail.

Among the natives that haunt the hotel are the snake charmers. They are almost naked fellows, sometimes with ragged jackets on and sometimes turbans on their heads, but more often the head is bare. They execute a number of tricks in a very skillful manner. The most wonderful of these tricks, to me, was that of growing a tree. They would show a seed, then they would place the seed on the ground, cover it with a handful of earth, and cover this little mound with a handkerchief, which they first passed around to be examined, that we might be positive there was nothing wrong with it. Over this they would chant, and after a time the handkerchief is taken off and then up through the ground is a green sprout. We look at it incredulously, while the man says:

"Tree no good; tree too small," and covering it up again he renews his chanting. Once more he lifts the handkerchief and we see the sprout is larger, but still it does not please the trickster, for he repeats: "Tree no good; tree too small," and covers it up again. This is repeated until he has a tree from three to five feet in height. Then he pulls it up, shows us the seed and roots.

Although these men always asked us to "See the snake dance?" we always saw every other trick but the one that had caught us. One morning, when a man urged me to "See the snake dance?" I said that I would, but that I would pay to see the snake dance and for nothing else. Quite unwillingly the men lifted the lid of the basket, and the cobra crawled slowly out, curling itself up on the ground. The "charmer" began to play on a little fife, meanwhile waving a red cloth which attracted the cobra's attention. It rose up steadily, darting angrily at the red cloth, and rose higher at every motion until it seemed to stand on the tip end of its tail. Then it saw the charmer and it darted for him, but he cunningly caught it by the head and with such a grip that I saw the blood gush from the snake's month. He worked for some time, still firmly holding the snake by the head before he could get it into the basket, the reptile meanwhile lashing the ground furiously with its tail. When at last it was covered from sight, I drew a long breath, and the charmer said to me sadly:

"Cobra no dance, cobra too young, cobra too fresh!"

I thought quite right; the cobra was too fresh!

At Colombo I saw the jinricksha for the first time. The jinricksha is a small two-wheel wagon, much in shape like a sulky, except that it has a top which can be raised in rainy weather. It has long shafts joined at the end with a crossbar. The jinricksha men are black and wear little else than a sash. When the sun is hot they wear large hats that look like enormous mushrooms, but most of the time these hats are hanging to the back of the 'ricksha. There are stands at different places for these men as well as carriage stands. While waiting for patrons they let their 'rickshas rest on the shafts and they sit in the bottom, their feet on the ground. Besides dressing in a sash these men dress in an oil or grease, and when the day is hot and they run, one wishes they wore more clothing and less oil! The grease has an original odor that is entirely its own.

One day I was going out in a 'ricksha and an acquaintance was going with me. The man put his foot on the shaft when I got in, and as he raised it, ready to start, I saw my friend step into her 'ricksha. She sat down and instantly went out—the other way! The man did not have his foot on the shaft and she overbalanced.

I had a shamed feeling about going around the town drawn by a man, but after I had gone a short way, I decided it was a great improvement on modern means of travel; it was so comforting to have a horse that was able to take care of itself! When we went into the shops it was so agreeable not to have the worry of fearing the horses were not blanketed, and when we made them run we did not have to fear we might urge them into a damaging speed. It is a great relief to have a horse whose tongue can protest.

I have spoken about the perfect roads in Ceylon. I found the roads in the same state of perfection in almost all the Eastern ports at which I stopped. I could not decide, to my own satisfaction, whether the smoothness of the road was due to the entire and blessed absence of beer wagons, or to the absence of the New York street commissioners.

I visited at the temples in Colombo, finding little of interest, and always having to pay liberally for the privilege of looking about. One day I went to the Buddhist college, and while there I met the famous high priest of Ceylon. He was sitting on a verandah, that surrounded his low bungalow, writing on a table placed before him. His gown consisted of a straight piece of old gold silk wrapped deftly around the body and over the waist. The silk had fallen to his waist, but after he greeted us he pulled it up around his shoulders. He was a copper-colored old fellow, with gray hair that was shaved very close to the head. He spoke English quite well, and among other things told me he received hundreds of letters from the United States every year, and that they found more converts to the Buddhist religion in America than in any other land.

The two newspapers in Colombo are in charge of two young Englishmen who are very clever. They are very kind to strangers, and I am indebted to them for a great deal of pleasure during my stay in Ceylon. The hotel manager is a German of high birth. He is untiring in his efforts to make his guests comfortable. His wife is a very pretty little woman, with a beautiful voice. Through her kindness I learned of a tailor in Ceylon who makes gowns, that for style and fit are not excelled. I have seen gowns from Worth that could not equal them, and this man charges for making a gown, five rupees! Five rupees are about two dollars and a half. He will make a gown in two days.

The praises of Kandy had been sung to me, so one morning at seven o'clock I started for Kandy with the Spanish representative, who was going to Pekin, and a jolly Irish lad who was bound for Hong Kong, both of whom had traveled with me from Brindisi. We drove to the station and were passed with the people, through the gate to the train. English cars, and ones that leave everything to be desired, are used on this line. We got into a compartment where there was but one seat, which, luckily for us, happened to be facing the way we traveled. Our tickets were taken at the station, and then the doors were locked and the train started. Before the start, we had entered our names in a book which a guard brought to us with the information that we could have breakfast on the train if so desired. As it was too early for breakfast at the hotel, we were only too glad to get an opportunity to eat. At eight o'clock the train stopped and the guard unlocked our door, telling us to go front to the dining-car. It seemed strange to be compelled to get out of a train, instead of walking through it, in order to get to the other end of it.

The dining-car was fitted up with stationary tables which almost spanned the car, leaving a small space for people to walk along. There were more people than could be accommodated, but as the train had started, they were obliged to stand. Several persons had told me that the breakfast served on this train was considered remarkably good. I thought, on seeing the bill of fare, they had prepared a feast for a chicken hawk. First, there was fish dressed in vinegar and onions, followed by chicken soup, chicken aspic, grilled chicken, boned chicken, fried chicken, boiled chicken, cold chicken and chicken pie!

After we had finished our breakfast we were compelled to remain where we were until the train arrived at some station. Then the dining-car was unlocked and we returned to the other car, being again locked in until the end of our journey. The road to Kandy is spoken of as being very beautiful. It winds up the mountain side and is rather pretty, but nothing wonderful in that respect. It is a tropical land, but the foliage and flowers are very ordinary. About the prettiest things to be seen are the rice beds. They are built in terraces, and when one looks down into the deep valley, seeing terrace after terrace of the softest, lightest green, one is forced to cry: "How beautiful!"

Arriving at Kandy at last, we hired a carriage and went to see the lake, the public library and the temples. In one old temple, surrounded by a moat, we saw several altars, of little consequence, and a bit of ivory which they told us was the tooth of Buddha. Kandy is pretty, but far from what it is claimed to be. They said it was cool, but we found it so hot that we thought with regret of Colombo. Disgusted with all we found worth seeing we drove to Parathenia to see the great botanical garden. It well repaid us for the visit. That evening we returned to Colombo. I was tired and hungry and the extreme heat had given me a sick headache. On the way down, the Spanish gentlemen endeavored to keep our falling spirits up, but every word he said only helped to increase my bad temper, much to the amusement of the Irish boy. He was very polite and kind, the Spaniard, I mean, but he had an unhappy way of flatly contradicting one, that, to say the least, was very exasperating. It was to me, but it only made the Irish boy laugh. When we were going down the mountain side the Spaniard got up, and standing, put his head through the open window in the door to get a view of the country.

"We are going over," he said, with positive conviction, turning around to us. I was leaning up in a corner trying to sleep and the Irish boy, with his feet braced against the end of the compartment, was trying to do the same.

"We won't go over," I managed to say, while the Irish boy smiled.

"Yes, we will," the Spaniard shouted back, "Make your prayers!"

The Irish boy screamed with laughter, and I forgot my sickness as I held my sides and laughed. It was a little thing, but it is often little things that raise the loudest laughs. After that all I needed to say to upset the dignity of the Irish boy was: "Make your prayers!"

I went to bed that night too ill to eat my dinner. The next morning I had intended to go to the pearl market, but felt unequal to it, and when my acquaintances returned and told me that at the very end of the sale a man bought some left over oysters for one rupee and found in them five hundred dollars worth of pearls, I felt sorry that I had not gone, although there was great danger of getting cholera.

One day I heard a man ask another if he knew the meaning of the word "jinricksha." the first replied the word meant "Draw man power," and the second said, with innocent surprise, "I thought it was 'Pull man car!'" I heard a passenger who came ashore from an Australian boat ask Andrew, a clever native who stands at the hotel door, to get him one of those carts to take a ride. Andrew did not know just what the man wanted as there were many different kinds of carts about.

"I don't recall the name of them," the passenger said, in a hesitating manner, "but I believe you call them Jim-Jams!"

He got a jinricksha.

X

IN THE PIRATE SEAS

One night, after I had been five days in Colombo, the blackboard in the hotel corridor bore the information that the Oriental would sail for China the following morning, at eight o'clock. I was called at five o'clock and some time afterwards left for the ship. The "Spanish minister," as we called the Spaniard, wanted me to go to some of the shops with him until he should buy some jewelry, but I was so nervous and anxious to be on my way that I could not wait a moment longer than was necessary to reach the boat that was to carry me to China.

When farewells had been said, and I was on the Oriental, I found my patience had given way under the long delay. The ship seemed to be deserted when I went on deck, with the exception of a handsome, elderly man, accompanied by a young blonde man in a natty white linen suit, who slowly promenaded the deck, watching out to sea while they talked. I was trying to untie my steamer chair so as to have some place to sit, when the elderly man came up and politely offered to assist me.

"When will we sail," I asked shortly.

"As soon as the Nepaul comes in," the man replied. "She was to have been here at daybreak, but she hasn't been sighted yet. Waiting for the Nepaul has given us this five days' delay. She's a slow old boat."

"May she go to the bottom of the bay when she does get in!" I said savagely. "The old tub! I think it an outrage to be kept waiting five days for a tub like that."

"Colombo is a pleasant place to stay," the elderly man said with a twinkle in his eye.

"It may be, if staying there does not mean more than life to one. Really, it would afford me the most intense delight to see the Nepaul go the bottom of the sea."

Evidently my ill humor surprised them, and their surprise amused me, for I thought how little anyone could realize what this delay meant to me, and the mental picture of a forlorn little self creeping back to New York ten days behind time, with a shamed look on her face and afraid to hear her name spoken, made me laugh outright. They gazed at me in astonishment, while I laughed immoderately at my own unenviable position. My better nature surged up with the laugh, and I was able to say, once again: "Everything happens for the best."

"There is the Nepaul," I said, pointing out a line of smoke just visible above the horizon. They doubted it, but a few moments proved that I was correct. "I am very ill-natured," I said, glancing from the kindly blue eyes of the elderly man to the laughing blue eyes of the younger man; "but I could not help it. After being delayed for five days I was called at five o'clock because they said the ship was to sail at eight, and here it is nine o'clock and there's no sign of the ship sailing and—I am simply famished."

As they laughed at my woes the gong sounded for breakfast and they took me down. The Irish lad, with his sparkling eyes and jolly laugh, was there, as was a young Englishman who had also traveled on the ship Victoria to Colombo. I knew him by sight, but as he was a sworn woman-hater I did not dare to speak to him. There were no women on board. I was the only woman that morning, and a right jolly breakfast we had.

The captain, a most handsome man, and as polite and courteous as he was good looking, sat at the head of the table. Officers, that any ship might boast of, were gathered about him. Handsome, good natured, intelligent, polite, they were, every single one of them. I found the elderly man I had been talking to was the chief engineer, and the young man was the ship's doctor.

The dining-hall was very artistic and pleasant, and the food was good. The ship, although much smaller than the Victoria, was very much better in every way. The cabins were more comfortable, the ship was better ventilated, the food was vastly superior, the officers were polite and good natured, the captain was a gentleman in looks and manners, and everything was just as agreeable as it could be. For several days I let things go on and said nothing about myself, nor did I give them the letter which the London agent had kindly sent. It had brought me no attention or courtesy on the Victoria, and I decided to take my chances on the Oriental. When I saw that uniform kindness and politeness was the rule on this ship, I then gave them the letter, and though the captain was pleased to receive it, still, it could not have made his treatment of me any kinder than it was at first.

It was well on to one o'clock before the passengers were transferred from the Nepaul to the Oriental. In the meantime the ship was amply peopled with merchants from the shore, who were selling jewels and lace. How they did cheat the passengers! They would ask, and sometimes get, fabulous prices for things, and when the ship was ready to sail, they offered to sell at any price. They were quite saucy chaps, too. I heard a vender reply to a man who offered him a small price for some so-called precious stones:

"I am not charging you for looking at these."

In fact they grew so impudent and bold, that I am surprised that the steamship lines do not issue orders prohibiting their presence on board.

At one o'clock we sailed. The first day and the two days following were passed lazily on deck. I found it a great relief to be again on the sweet, blue sea, out of sight of land, and free from the tussle and worry and bustle for life which we are daily, hourly even, forced to gaze upon on land. Although the East is, in a very great measure, free from the dreadful crowding for life, still one is bound to see signs of it even among the most indolent of people. Only on the bounding blue, the grand, great sea, is one rocked into a peaceful rest at noon of day, at dusk of night, feeling that one is drifting, drifting, not seeing, or knowing, or caring, about fool mortals striving for life. True, the sailors do this and that, but it has an air far from that of elbowing each other for a living. To the lazy passengers it seems that they merely hoist a sail or pull it down, that they may drift—dream—sleep—talk—live for happiness and not for gain.

The fourth day out was Sunday. The afternoon was spent on deck looking at the most beautiful green islands which we slowly passed. Sometimes we would lazily conjecture as to whether they were inhabited or not.

The next day we anchored at Penang, or Prince of Wales Island, one of the Straits Settlements. As the ship had such a long delay at Colombo, it was said that we would have but six hours to spend on shore. With an acquaintance as escort, I made my preparations and was ready to go to land the moment we anchored. We went ashore in a Sampan, an oddly shaped flat boat with the oars, or rather paddles, fastened near the stern. The Malay oarsman rowed hand over hand, standing upright in the stern, his back turned towards us as well as the way we were going. Frequently he turned his head to see if the way was clear, plying his oars industriously all the while. Once landed he chased us to the end of the pier demanding more money, although we had paid him thirty cents, just twenty cents over and above the legal fare.

Hiring a carriage we drove to where a waterfall comes bounding down the side of a naturally verdant mountain which has been transformed, half way up, into a pleasing tropical garden. The picturesque waterfall is nothing marvelous. It only made me wonder from whence it procured its water supply, but after walking until I was much heated, and finding myself apparently just as far from the fount, I concluded the waterfall's secret was not worth the fatigue it would cost.

On the way to the town we visited a Hindoo temple. Scarcely had we entered when a number of half-clad, bare-footed priests rushed frantically upon us, demanding that we remove our shoes. The temple being built open, its curved roof and rafters had long been utilized by birds and pigeons as a bed-room. Doubtless ages had passed over the stone floor, but I could swear nothing else had, so I refused emphatically and unconditionally to un-boot myself. I saw enough of their idols to satisfy me. One was a black god in a gay dress, the other was a shapeless black stone hung with garlands of flowers, the filthy stone at its base being buried 'neath a profusion of rich blossoms.

English is spoken less in Penang than in any port I visited. A native photographer, when I questioned him about it, said:

"The Malays are proud, Miss. They have a language of their own and they are too proud to speak any other."

That photographer knew how to use his English to advantage. He showed me cabinet-sized proofs for which he asked one dollar each.

"One dollar!" I exclaimed in astonishment, "That is very high for a proof."

"If Miss thinks it is too much she does not need to buy. She is the best judge of how much she can afford to spend," he replied with cool impudence.

"Why are they so expensive?" I asked, nothing daunted by his impertinence.

"I presume because Penang is so far from England," he rejoined, carelessly.

I was told afterwards that a passenger from the Oriental pulled the photographer's long, thin, black nose for his impudence, and I was pleased to hear it.

A Chinese joss-house, the first I had seen, was very interesting. The pink and white roof, curved like a canoe, was ornamented with animals of the dragon tribe, with their mouths open and their tails in the air. The straggling worshippers could be plainly seen from the streets through the arcade sides of the temple. Chinese lanterns and gilt ornaments made gay the dark interior. Little josses, with usual rations of rice, roast pig and smouldering joss-sticks disbursing a strangely sweet perfume, were no more interesting than a dark corner in which the superstitious were trying their luck, a larger crowd of dusky people than were about the altars. In fact, the only devoutee was a waxed-haired Chinese woman, with a slit-eyed brown babe tied on her back, bowing meekly and lowly before a painted, be-bangled joss.

Some priests with shaven heads and old-gold silk garments, who were in a summer-house in the garden, saw us when we were looking at the gold-fish ponds. One came forth, and, taking me by the hand, gracefully led me to where they were gathered. They indicated their wish that we should sit with them and drink tea with them, milkless and sugarless, from child-like China cups, which they re-filled so often that I had reasons for feeling thankful the cups were so like unto play-dishes. We were unable to exchange words, but we smiled liberal smiles, at one another.

Mexican silver is used almost exclusively in Penang. American silver will be accepted at the same value, but American gold is refused and paper money is looked on with contempt. The Chinese jinricksha men in Penang, compared with those in Colombo, are like over-fed pet horses besides racers in trim. They were the plumpest Chinamen I ever saw; such round fat legs and arms!

When we started back to the ship the bay was very rough. Huge waves angrily tossed our small boat about in a way that blotted the red from my escort's checks and caused him to hang his head in a care-for-nothing way over the boat's side. I could not help liking the sea to a coquette, so indifferent and heedless is it to the strange emotions it raises in the breast of man. It was a reckless spring that landed us on the ship's ladder, the rolling of the coal barge helping to increase the swell which had threatened to engulf us. Hardly had we reached deck when the barge was ordered to cut loose; even as this was being done the ship hoisted anchor and started on its way. Almost immediately there was a great commotion on board. About fifty ragged black men rushed frantically on deck to find that while depositing their last sacks of coal in the regions below, their barge and companions had cast off and were rapidly nearing the shore. Then followed dire chattering, wringing of hands, pulling of locks and crying after the receding barge, all to no avail. The tide was coming in, a very strong tide it was, too, and despite the efforts of those on it the barge was steadily swept inland.

The captain appeased the coolies' fears by stating that they should go off in the pilot's boat. We all gathered to see the sight and a funny one it was! The tug being lashed to the ship they first tried to take the men off without slowing down but after one man got a dangerous plunge bath and the sea threatened to bury the tug then the ship was forced to slow down. Some coolies slid down a cable, their comrades grabbing and pulling them wet and frightened white on to the tug. Others went down the ladder which lacked five feet of touching the pilot boat. Those already on board would clutch the hanging man's bare legs, he meanwhile clinging despairingly to the ladder, fearing to loosen his grasp and only doing so when the ship officers would threaten to knock him off.

The pilot, a native, was the last to go down. Then the cable was cast off and we sailed away seeing the tug, so overloaded that the men were afraid to move even to bail it out, swept back by the tide towards the place where we had last seen the land.

I had a cabin down below at first and I found little rest owing to the close proximity of a nurse and two children whose wise parents selected a cabin on the other side of the ship. They could rest in peace. After I had been awakened several mornings at daybreak by the squabbling of the children I cherished a grudge against the parents. The mother made some show of being a beauty. She had a fine nose, everybody confessed that, and she had reduced her husband to such a state of servitude and subjection that she needed no maids.

I have always confessed that I like to sleep in the morning as well as I like to stay up at night, and to have my sleep disturbed makes me as ill-natured as a bad dinner makes a man. The fond father of these children had a habit of coming over early in the morning to see his cherubs, before he went to his bath. I know this from hearing him tell them so. He would open their cabin door and in the loudest, coldest, most unsympathetic voice in the world, would thoroughly arouse me from my slumbers by screaming:

"Good morning. How is papa's family this morning?"

A confused conglomeration of voices sounded in reply; then he would shout:

"What does baby say to mamma? Say; what does baby say to mamma?"

"Mamma!" baby would at length shout back in a coarse, unnatural baby voice.

"What does baby say to papa? Tell me, baby, what does baby say to papa?"

"Papa!" would answer back the shrill treble.

"What does the moo-moo cow say, my treasure; tell papa what the moo-moo cow says?"

To this the baby would make no reply and again he would shout:

"What does the moo-moo cow say, darling; tell papa what the moo-moo cow says?"

If it had been once, or twice even, I might have endured it with civilized forbearance but after it had been repeated, the very same identical word every morning for six long weary mornings, my temper gave way and when he said: "Tell papa what the moo-moo cow says?" I shouted frantically:

"For heaven's sake, baby, tell papa what the moo-moo cow says and let me go to sleep."

A heavy silence, a silence that was heavy with indignation and surprise, followed and I went off to sleep to dream of being chased down a muddy hill by babies sitting astride cows with crumpled horns, and straight horns and no horns at all, all singing in a melodious cow-like voice, moo! moo! moo!

The fond parents did not speak to me after that. They gazed on me in disdain and when the woman got sea-sick I persuaded an acquaintance of hers to go in and see her one day by telling her it was her Christian duty. The fond mother would not allow the ship doctor to see her although her husband had to relate her ills to the doctor and in that way get him to prescribe for them. I knew there was something she wished to keep secret. The woman, true to my counsel, knocked on the door; hearing no voice and thinking it lost in the roar of the ocean opened the door. The fond mother looked up, saw, and screaming buried her face in the pillows, She was toothless and hairless! The frightened Samaritan did not wait to see if she had a cork limb! I felt repentant afterwards and went to a deck cabin where I soon forgot the moo-moo cow and the fond parents. But the woman's fame as a beauty was irrevocably ruined on the ship.

It was so damply warm in the Straits of Malacca that for time first time during my trip I confessed myself uncomfortably hot. It was sultry and foggy and so damp that everything rusted, even the keys in one's pockets, and the mirrors were so sweaty that they ceased to reflect. The second day out from Penang we passed beautiful green islands. There were many stories told about the straits being once infested with pirates, and I regretted to hear that they had ceased to exist, I so longed for some new experience.

We expected to reach Singapore that night. I was anxious that we should, for the sooner we got in the sooner we should leave, and every hour lost meant so much to me. The pilot came on at six o'clock. I waited tremblingly for his verdict. A wave of despair swept over me when I heard that we should anchor outside until morning, because it was too dangerous to try to make the port after dark. And this was the result of slowing down to leave off the coolies at Penang. The mail contract made it compulsory for the ship to stay in port twenty-four hours, and while we might have been consuming our stay and so helping me on in my race against time I was wasting precious hours lying outside the gates of hope, as it were, merely because some black men had been too slow. Those few hours might mean time loss of my ship at Hong Kong; they might mean days to my record. What agony of suspense and impatience I suffered that night!

When I came on deck time next morning the ship lay along side the wharf, and naked Chinese coolies carrying, two by two, baskets of coal suspended between them on a pole, were constantly traversing the gang-plank between the ship and shore, while in little boats about were peddlers with silks, photographs, fruits, laces and monkeys to sell.

The doctor, a young Welshman, and I hired a gharry, a light wagon with latticed windows and comfortable seating room for four with the driver's seat on the same level outside. They are drawn by a pretty spotted Malay pony whose speed is marvelous compared with its diminutive size, and whose endurance is of such quality that the law confines their working hours to a certain limit.

Driving along a road as smooth as a ball-room floor, shaded by large trees, made picturesque by native houses built on pins in marshy land on either side, which tended to dampen our surprise at the great number of graveyards and the generous way in which they were filled, we drove to the town. The graves were odd, being round mounds with walls shaped like horse-shoes. A flat stone where the mound ends and the wall begins bears the inscriptions done in colored letters.

There are no sidewalks in Singapore, and blue and white in the painting of the houses largely predominate over other colors. Families seem to occupy the second story, the lower being generally devoted to business purposes. Through latticed windows we got occasional glimpses of peeping Chinese women in gay gowns, Chinese babies bundled in shapeless, wadded garments, while down below through widely opened fronts we could see people pursuing their trades. Barbering is the principal trade. A chair, a comb, a basin and a knife are all the tools a man needs to open shop, and he finds as many patrons if he sets up shop in the open street as he would under shelter. Sitting doubled over, Chinamen have their heads shaven back almost to the crown, when a spot about the size of a tiny saucer is left to bear the crop of hair which forms the pig-tail. When braided and finished with a silk tassel the Chinaman's hair is "done" for the next fortnight.

The people here, as at other ports where I stopped, constantly chew betel nut, and when they laugh one would suppose they had been drinking blood. The betel nut stains their teeth and mouthfuls blood-red. Many of the natives also fancy tinting their finger-nails with it.

Nothing is patronized more than the 'rickshas in Singapore, and while they are to be had for ten cents an hour it is no unusual sight to see four persons piled in one jinricksha and drawn by one man. We visited a most interesting museum, and saw along the suburban roads the beautiful bungalows of the European citizens. People in dog-carts and wheelmen on bicycles crowded the splendid drives.

We found the monkey-cage, of course. There was besides a number of small monkeys one enormous orang-outang. It was as large as a man and was covered with long red hair. While seeming to be very clever he had a way of gazing off in the distance with wide, unseeing eyes, meanwhile pulling his long red hair up over his head in an aimless, insane way that was very fetching. The doctor wanted to give him a nut, but feared to put his hand through the bars. The grating was too small for the old fellow to get his hand through, but he did not intend to be cheated of his rights, so he merely stuck his lips through the gratings until they extended fully four inches. I burst into laughter at the comical sight. I had heard of mouths, but that beat anything I ever saw, and I laughed until the old fellow actually smiled in sympathy. He got the nut!

The doctor offered him a cigar. He did not take it, but touched it with the back of his hand, afterwards smelling his hand, and then subsided into that dreamy state, aimlessly pulling his hair up over the back of his head.

At the cable office, in the second story of a building, I found the agents conversant with the English language. They would accept American silver at par, but they did not care to handle our other money. The bank and post-office are open places on the ground floor with about as much comfort and style as is found in ordinary wharf warehouses. Chinese and English are employed in both places.

We had dinner at the Hotel de l'Europe, a long, low, white building set back in a wide, green lawn, with a beautiful esplanade, faced by the sea, fronting it. Upon the verandah were long white tables where a fine dinner was served by Chinamen.

On our return from the Governor's House, I heard a strange, weird din as of many instruments in dire confusion and discord, very like in sound to a political procession the night after the presidential election.

"That's a funeral," my Malay driver announced.

"Indeed! If that is the way you have funerals here, I'll see one," I said. So he pulled the gharry to one side where we waited eagerly for a funeral that was heralded by a blast of trumpets. First came a number of Chinamen with black and white satin flags which, being flourished energetically, resulted in clearing the road of vehicles and pedestrians. They were followed by musicians on Malay ponies, blowing fifes, striking cymbals, beating tom-toms, hammering gongs, and pounding long pieces of iron, with all their might and main. Men followed carrying on long poles roast pigs and Chinese lanterns, great and small, while in their rear came banner-bearers. The men on foot wore white trousers and sandals, with blue top dress, while the pall-bearers wore black garments bound with blue braid. There were probably forty pall-bearers. The casket, which rested on long poles suspended on the shoulders of the men, was hidden beneath a white-spotted scarlet cloth with decorations of Chinese lanterns or inflated bladders on arches above it. The mourners followed in a long string of gharries, They were dressed in white satin from head to toe and were the happiest looking people at the funeral. We watched until the din died away in the distance when we returned to town as delighted as if we had seen a circus parade.

"I would not have missed that for anything," Doctor Brown said to me.

"You could not," I replied laughingly, "I know they got it up for our special benefit."

And so laughing and jesting about what had to us no suggestion of death, we drove back to see the temples. None of us were permitted to pass beneath the gate of the Mahommedan temple, so we went on to a Hindoo temple. It was a low stone building, enclosed by a high wall. At the gateway leading to it were a superfluity of beggars, large and small, lame and blind, who asked for alms, touching their foreheads respectfully. The temple was closed but some priests rushed forth to warn us not step on the sacred old dirty stone-passage leading to it with our shoes on. Its filth would have made it sacred to me with my shoes off! My comrades were told that removing their shoes would give them admission but I should be denied that privilege because I was a woman.

"Why?" I demanded, curious to know why my sex in heathen lands should exclude me from a temple, as in America it confines me to the side entrances of hotels and other strange and incommodious things.

"No, Señora, no mudder," the priest said with a positive shake of the head.

"I'm not a mother!" I cried so indignantly that my companions burst into laughter, which I joined after a while, but my denials had no effect on the priest. He would not allow me to enter.

In some sheds which lined the inner part of the high wall we saw a number of fantastically shaped carts of heavy build. Probably they were juggernauts. Near by we saw through the bars a wooden image of a woman. Her shape was neither fairy-like nor girlish; her features were fiendish in expression and from her mouth fell a long string of beads. As the mother of a poor man's family she would have been a great success. Instead of one pair of arms she had four. One pair was employed in holding a stiff wooden baby before her and the other three pairs were taking care of themselves much like the legs of a crab. They showed us a white wooden horse mounted on wheels, images of most horrible devils, in short, we saw so many images of such horrible shapes that it would be impossible to recall them all. I remember one head that I was very much interested in and the limited English of the priest failed to satisfy my curiosity as to who, what, and for what purpose the thing was invented.

It was only a head but must have been fully twelve feet high and wide in proportion. The face was a fiery scarlet and the eyes were tightly closed. On the lawn, fastened to a slight pin, was a white cow, the only presentable cow I saw during my trip.

I noticed the doctor gave her wide range keeping his eye on her as she playfully tossed her head.

"Be careful," he said nervously to me. "I believe that's the sacred white cow."

"She looks old enough—and tough enough—to make her sacred in the eye of a butcher!" I replied.

"If she is the sacred cow," he continued, despite my levity, "and went for us they would consider it their duty to let the old beast kill an infidel. That pin does not look very strong."

So to quiet the fears of the doctor we left the old cow and the gods behind.

The people in Singapore have ranks as have people in other lands. There they do not wait for one neighbor to tell another or for the newspapers to inform the public as to their standing but every man, woman, and child carries his mark in gray powder on the forehead so that all the world may look and read and know his caste.

We stopped at the driver's humble home on our way to the ship and I saw there on the ground floor, his pretty little Malay wife dressed in one wrapping of linen, and several little brown naked babies. The wife had a large gold ring in her nose, rings on her toes and several around the rim of her ears, and gold ornaments on her ankles. At the door of their home was a monkey. I did resist the temptation to buy a boy at Port Said and also smothered the desire to buy a Singalese girl at Colombo, but when I saw the monkey my will-power melted and I began straightway to bargain for it. I got it.

"Will the monkey bite?" I asked the driver, and he took it by the throat, holding it up for me to admire as he replied:

"Monkey no bite." But he could not under the circumstances.

XI

Against the Monsoon

That evening we sailed for Hong Kong. The next day the sea was rough and head winds made the run slower than we had hoped for. Towards noon almost all the passengers disappeared. The roughness increased and the cook enjoyed a holiday. There was some chaffing among the passengers who remained on deck. During dinner the chief officer began to relate the woes of people he had seen suffering from the dire disease that threatened now to even overpower the captain. I listened for quite a while, merely because I could not help hearing; and if there was anything the chief could do well it was relating anecdotes. At last one made me get up and run, it was so vivid, and the moment the doctor, who sat opposite, saw me go he got up and followed. I managed to overcome my faintness without really being sick, but the doctor gave way entirely. I went back to dinner to find the cause of our misery had disappeared. When I saw him later, his face was pale and he confessed contritely that his realistic joke had made even him seasick.

During the roughness that followed the doctor would always say to me pleadingly:

"Don't make a start, for if you do I will have to follow."

The terrible swell of the sea during the Monsoon was the most beautiful thing I ever saw. I would sit breathless on deck watching the bow of the ship standing upright on a wave then dash headlong down as if intending to carry us to the bottom. Some of the men made no secret of being seasick and were stretched out in their chairs on deck where they might hope to catch the first breath of air. Although there was a dreadful swell, still the atmosphere was heavy and close. Sometimes I felt as if I would smother. One man who had been quite attentive to me became seasick. I was relieved when I heard it, still I felt very cruel when I would see his pale face and hear him plead for sympathy. As heartless as I thought it was I could not sympathize with a seasick man. There was an effort on the part of others to tease the poor fellow. When I sat down on deck they would carefully take away all the chairs excepting those occupied by themselves, but it mattered little to the seasick man. He would quietly curl up on his rugs at my feet and there lie, in all his misery, gazing at me.

"You would not think that I am enjoying a vacation, but I am," he said plaintively to me one day.

"You don't know how nice I can look," he said pathetically at another time. "If you would only stay over at Hong Kong for a week you would see how pretty I can look."

"Indeed, such a phenomenon might induce me to remain there six weeks," I said coldly.

At last some one told him I was engaged to the chief officer, who did not approve of my talking to other men, thinking this would make him cease following me about, but it only served to increase his devotion. Finding me alone on deck one stormy evening he sat down at my feet and holding to the arms of my chair began to talk in a wild way.

"Do you think life is worth living?" he asked.

"Yes, life is very sweet. The thought of death is the only thing that causes me unhappiness," I answered truthfully.

"You cannot understand it or you would feel different. I could take you in my arms and jump overboard, and before they would know it we would be at rest," he said passionately.

"You can't tell. It might not be rest—" I began and he broke in hotly.

"I know, I know. I can show you. I will prove it to you. Death by drowning is a peaceful slumber, a quiet drifting away."

"Is it?" I said, with a pretense of eagerness. I feared to get up for I felt the first move might result in my burial beneath the angry sea.

"You know, tell me about it. Explain it to me," I gasped, a feeling of coldness creeping over me as I realized that I was alone with what for the time was a mad man. Just as he began to speak I saw the chief officer come on deck and slowly advance towards me. I dared not call. I dared not smile, lest he should notice. I feared the chief would go away, but no, he saw me, and with a desire to tease the man who had been so devoted he came up on tip-toe, then, clapping the poor fellow on the back, he said: "What a very pretty love scene!"

"Come," I shouted, breaking away before the startled man could understand. The chief, still in a spirit of fun, took my hand and we rushed down below. I told him and the captain what had occurred and the captain wanted to put the man in irons but I begged that he be left free. I was careful afterwards not to spend one moment alone and unprotected on deck.

The Parsees, traveling first class, were compelled to go below when a heavy swell was on. We welcomed the storm on that account if on no other, because they had a peculiar habit of dropping off their slippers when they sat down. As they wore no hose, this habit was annoying.

The doctor seriously affirmed that every time he sat down anywhere a Parsee was sure to squat alongside, drop his shoes and turn his bare, brown feet up to be gazed upon.

The monkey proved a good seaman. One day when I visited it I found the young men had been toasting its health. It was holding its aching head when I went in, and evidently thinking I was the cause of the swelling, it sprang at me, making me seek safety in flight.

The hurricane deck was a great resort for lovers, so Chief Officer Sleeman told me; and evidently he knew, for he talked a great deal about two American girls who had traveled to Egypt, I believe, on the Thames when he was first officer of it. He had lost their address but his heart was true, for he had lost a philopoena to one and though he did not know her habitation he bought the philopoena and put it in a bank in London where it awaits some farther knowledge of the fair young American's whereabouts.

Lovers were not plentiful on the Oriental, there were so few passengers. The "Spanish minister" had an eye for beauty and a heart for romance, though he led a most quiet life on shipboard, and was the very essence of gallantry.

"I was very much in love with a woman once. Traveling on the same ship with me was a woman, a beautiful woman, most beautiful, indeed. I watched her, she watched me, and my eyes told her I admired her and her eyes said back to me they were pleased that it should be so. Two men were traveling with her. One day I awkwardly knocked against her in a corridor and I said, 'I beg your pardon, Miss!' To which she answered lowly and sadly: 'I beg Your pardon,—*Mrs!*' When she came to dinner that night her eyes were red from weeping. I caught her glance; it spoke so sadly to me, her lips trembling like a grieved child's. She started in to drink a great deal of wine but one look from me made her push her glass away. Her husband, for she was married, was a very brutal fellow and my love for the beautiful woman almost made me forget my family and hers in my longing to claim her as my heart's companion. They left us at the first port. I stood on deck as they came up to go ashore. Her husband and his comrade went down the steps. Starting to follow she saw me, and stopped. Her eyes said to me as plain as speech, 'Say but the word and I am yours,' and although my feelings made me spring towards her, I paused before touching her and my aching eyes said: 'Go! be a good woman.' She went slowly down into the boat. Rising to her feet as it moved off, she held out her arms to me and with a great despairing cry fell back in the boat insensible! I never saw her since, I never knew her name, but I know as well as I know you are there that beautiful woman loved me!"

"And you?" I said inquiringly.

"I!" with a slight shrug of the shoulders, accompanied by a little cold laugh, which was not unpleasant to hear; it somehow reminded me of the sound of dripping water on a hot day. "Ah, she was a beautiful lady, very, ver-ry beautiful, most beautiful, indeed, but Señorita, I have a son older than you and I am devoted to my family."

Impatiently I turned to an Englishman who was sitting on the other side.

"Why do Englishmen always say 'Deah me!'" I lazily asked.

"Deah me! Do they? I can't sai, don't you know."

"Well, I can. It's because they think so wonderfully much of themselves," I said with a laugh.

"Deah me! Really?" was all he said in reply.

"You are so jolly clever, now; can you tell me why Eve did not take the measles?" he asked after a time.

"'Cause she'd 'ad 'em" (Adam), I said in a Bowery tone.

"I sai, now, you are jolly clever, but can you tell me why Cain did not take them? Hasten, now, I cannot dwell."

"Because he wasn't Abel. Now don't dwell, but move on and tell me what chestnuts are?" I said, teasingly.

"Oh come, now—"

"I'm here."

"I sai, really, you Americans have such a jolly queer language. Deah me, I can't tell."

"I thought you could, you have such a jolly supply of them, 'don't you know.'"

"Deah me!" he exclaimed, as he rushed down below to brace on a whiskey and soda.

It is wonderful the amount of whiskey and soda Englishmen consume. They drink it at all times and places. There was an Englishman on the Oriental who drank whiskey and soda all the day, half a dozen different wines at dinner, and then complained, as he invariably staggered away from the table, that the wine list had no variety!

Talk about cranks! One woman told the chief officer one day that she wanted a cabin just over the ship's screw so she could tell that the ship was going! She got it, and she was the worst sea-sick woman I ever saw. Another passenger complained because the berths had spring mattresses!

One night during the monsoon the sea washed over the ship in a frightful manner. I found my cabin filled with water, which, however, did not touch my berth. Escape to the lower deck was impossible, as I could not tell the deck from the angry, pitching sea. As I crawled back into my bunk a feeling of awe crept over me and with it a conscious feeling of satisfaction. I thought it very possible that I had spoken my last word to any mortal, that the ship would doubtless sink, and with it all I thought, if the ship did go down, no one would be able to tell whether I could have gone around the world in seventy-five days or not. The thought was very comforting at that time, for I felt then I might not get around in one hundred days.

I could have worried myself over my impending fate had I not been a great believer in letting unchangeable affairs go their way. "If the ship does go down," I thought, "there is time enough to worry when it's going. All the worry in the world cannot change it one way or the other, and if the ship does not go down, I only waste so much time." So I went to sleep and slumbered soundly until the breakfast hour.

The ship was making its way laboriously through a very frisky sea when I looked out, but the deck was drained, even if it was not dry.

When I went out, the jolly Irish lad, for whom I had a great fondness, was stretched out languidly in a willow chair with a bottle of champagne on one arm-rest and a glass on the other. Every little motion of the ship made him vow that when he reached Hong Kong he would stay there until he could return to England overland!

"You should have seen my cabin-mate last night," he said with a laugh when I sat down beside him. The man he spoke of, a very clever Englishman, was the man who posed as a woman-hater, and naturally we enjoyed any joke at his expense.

"Finding our cabin filling with water, he got out of bed, put on a life preserver and bailed out the cabin with a cigarette box!"

I laughed until my sides ached at the mental picture presented to me of the little chunky Englishman in an enormous life preserver, bailing out his cabin with a tiny cigarette box! Even the box of the deadly cigarette seems to have its christian mission to perform. While I was wiping away the tears brought there by the strength of my laughter, the Englishman came up, and hearing what had amused us, said: "While

I was bailing out the cabin, 'the boy,' "as we fondly called him, "clung to the upper berth all the time groaning and praying! He was certain the ship would sink, and I could not persuade him to get out of the top berth to help bail. He would do nothing but groan and pray."

The boy answered with a laugh, "I did not want to sleep the rest of the night in wet pajamas," which caused the woman-hater to flee!

Later in the day the rolling was frightful. I was sitting on deck when all at once the ship went down at one side like a wagon in a deep rut. I was thrown in my chair clear across the deck. A young man endeavored to come to my assistance just as the ship went the other way in a still deeper sea-rut. It flung me back again, and only by catching hold of an iron bar did I save my neck at least, for in another moment I would have been dashed through the skylight into the dining hall on the deck below.

As I caught the bar, I saw the man who had rushed to my assistance turned upside down and land on his face. I began to laugh, his position was so ludicrous. When I saw he made no move to get up, I ran to his side, still convulsed with laughter. I found his nose was bleeding profusely, but I was such an idiot that the sight of the blood only served to make the scene to me the more ridiculous. Helping him to a chair, I ran for the doctor and from laughing could hardly tell him what I wanted. The man's nose was broken, and the doctor said he would be scarred for life. Even the others laughed when I described the accident, and, although I felt a great pity for the poor fellow, hurt as he was in my behalf, still an irresistible impulse to laugh would sweep over me every time I endeavored to express my appreciation of his attempt to assist me.

Our passengers were rather queer. I always enjoy the queerness of people. One day, when speaking about the boat, I said:

"Everything is such an improvement on the Victoria. The food is good, the passengers are refined, the officers are polite and the ship is comfortable and pleasant."

When I finished my complimentary remarks about the ship, a little bride who had been a source of interest to us looked up and said:

"Yes, everything is very nice; but the life preservers are not quite comfortable to sleep in."

Shocked amazement spread over the countenances of all the passengers, and then in one grand shout that dining-room resounded with laughter. The bride said that ever since they left home on their bridal tour they had been sleeping in the life preservers. They thought it was the thing to do on board a ship.

But I never knew how queer our passengers were until we reached Hong Kong, which we did two days ahead of time, although we had the monsoon against us. When we landed, a man sued the company for getting him in ahead of time. He said he bought his tickets to cover a certain length of time, and if the company got him in before it expired they were responsible for his expenses, and they had to pay his hotel bill.

The captain asked a minister who was on board to read the service one Sunday. He did so, and when he reached Hong Kong he put in a bill for two pounds! He said he was enjoying a vacation and did not propose to work during that time unless he was paid for it! The company paid, but warned the officers not to let ministers read the service thereafter until they knew their price.

The evening of December 22 we all sat on deck in a dark corner. The men were singing and telling stories. The only other woman who was able to be up and I were the interested and appreciative audience. We all felt an eagerness for morning and yet the eagerness was mingled with much that was sad. Knowing that early in the day we would reach Hong Kong, and while it would bring us new scenes and new acquaintances, it would take us from old friends.

XII

BRITISH CHINA

W e first saw the city of Hong Kong in the early morning. Gleaming white were the castle-like homes on the tall mountain side. We fired a cannon as we entered the bay, the captain saying that this was the custom of mail ships. A beautiful bay was this magnificent basin, walled on every side by high mountains. Once within this natural fortified harbor we could discern, in different directions, only small outlets between the mountains, but so small, indeed, they appeared that one could hardly believe a ship would find space large enough for passage. In fact, these outlets are said to be dangerously narrow, the most vigilant care being necessary until the ship is safely beyond on the ocean blue. Mirror-like was the bay in the bright sun, dotted with strange craft from many countries. Heavy iron-clads, torpedo boats, mall steamers, Portuguese lorchas, Chinese junks and sampans. Even as we looked, a Chinese ship wended its way slowly out to sea. Its queer, broad stern hoisted high out of the water and the enormous eye gracing its bow, were to us most interesting. A graceful thing I thought it, but I heard an officer call it most ungraceful and unshapely.

Hong Kong is strangely picturesque. It is a terraced city, the terraces being formed by the castle-like, arcaded buildings perched tier after tier up the mountain's verdant side. The regularity with which the houses are built in rows made me wildly fancy them a gigantic staircase, each stair made in imitation of castles.

The doctor, another gentleman, and I left the boat, and walking to the pier's end selected sedan chairs, in which we were carried to the town. The carriers were as urgent as our hackmen around railway stations in America. There is a knack of getting into a chair properly. It is placed upon the ground, the carrier tilts the shafts down, and the patron steps inside, back towards the chair, and goes into it backward. Once seated, the carriers hoist the chair to their shoulders and start off with a monotonous trot, which gives the chair a motion not unlike that of a pacing saddle-horse.

We followed the road along the shore, passing warehouses of many kinds and tall balconied buildings filled with hundreds of Chinese families, on the flat-house plan. The balconies would have lent a pleasing appearance to the houses had the inhabitants not seemed to be enjoying a washing jubilee, using the balconies for clotheslines. Garments were stretched on poles, after the manner of hanging coats so they will not wrinkle, and those poles were fastened to the balconies until it looked as if every family in the street had placed their old clothing on exhibition.

The town seemed in a state of untidiness, the road was dirty, the mobs of natives we met were filthy, the houses were dirty, the numberless boats lying along the wharf, which invariably were crowded with dirty people, were dirty, our carriers were dirty fellows, their untidy pig-tails twisted around their half-shaven heads. They trotted steadily ahead, snorting at the crowds of natives we met to clear the way. A series of snorts or grunts would cause a scattering of natives more frightened than a tie-walker would be at the tooting of an engine's whistle.

Turning off the shore road our carriers started up one of the roads which wind about from tier to tier up the mountain.

My only wish and desire was to get as speedily as possible to the office of the Oriental and Occidental Steamship Company to learn the earliest possible time I could leave for Japan, to continue my race against time around the world. I had just marked off my thirty-ninth day. Only thirty-nine days since leaving New York and I was in China. I was leaving particularly elated, because the good ship Oriental not only made up the five days I had lost in Colombo, but reached Hong Kong two days before I was due, according to my schedule. And that with the northeast monsoon against her. It was the Oriental's maiden trip to China, and from Colombo to Hong Kong she had broken all previous records.

I went to the O. and O. office feeling very much elated over my good fortune, with never a doubt but that it would continue.

"Will you tell me the date of the first sailing for Japan?" I asked a man in the office.

"In one moment," he said, and going into an inner office he brought out a man who looked at me inquiringly, and when I repeated my question, said:

"What is your name?"

"Nellie Bly," I replied in some surprise.

"Come in, come in," he said nervously. We followed him in, and after we were seated he said:

"You are going to be beaten."

"What? I think not. I have made up my delay," I said, still surprised, wondering if the Pacific had sunk since my departure from New York, or if all the ships on that line had been destroyed.

"You are going to lose it," he said with an air of conviction.

"Lose it? I don't understand. What do you mean?" I demanded, beginning to think he was mad.

"Aren't you having a race around the world?" he asked, as if he thought I was not Nellie Bly.

"Yes; quite right. I am running a race with Time," I replied.

"Time? I don't think that's her name."

"Her! Her!!" I repeated, thinking, "Poor fellow, he is quite unbalanced," and wondering if I dared wink at the doctor to suggest to him the advisability of our making good our escape.

"Yes, the other woman; she is going to win. She left here three days ago."

I stared at him; I turned to the doctor; I wondered if I was awake; I concluded the man was quite mad, so I forced myself to laugh in an unconcerned manner, but I was only able to say stupidly:

"The other woman?"

"Yes," he continued briskly; "Did you not know? The day you left New York another woman started out to beat your time, and she's going to do it. She left here three days ago. You probably met somewhere near the Straits of Malacca. She says she has authority to pay any amount to get ships to leave in advance of their time. Her editor offered one or two thousand dollars to the O. and O. if they would have the Oceanic leave San Francisco two days ahead of time. They would not do it, but they did do their best to get her here in time to catch the English mail for Ceylon. If they had not arrived long before they were due, she would have missed that boat, and so have been delayed ten days. But she caught the boat and left three days ago, and you will be delayed here five days."

"That is rather hard, isn't it?" I said quietly, forcing a smile that was on the lips, but came from nowhere near the heart.

"I'm astonished you did not know anything about it," he said. "She led us to suppose that it was an arranged race."

"I do not believe my editor would arrange a race without advising me," I said stoutly. "Have you no cables or messages for me from New York?"

"Nothing," was his reply.

"Probably they do not know about her," I said more cheerfully.

"Yes they do. She worked for the same newspaper you do until the day she started."

"I do not understand it," I said quietly, too proud to show my ignorance on a subject of vital importance to my well-doing. "You say I cannot leave here for five days?"

"No, and I don't think you can get to New York in eighty days. She intends to do it in seventy. She has letters to steamship officials at every point requesting them to do all they can to get her on. Have you any letters?"

"Only one, from the agent of the P. and O., requesting the captains of their boats to be good to me because I am traveling alone. That is all," I said with a little smile.

"Well, it's too bad; but I think you have lost it. There is no chance for you. You will lose five days here and five in Yokohoma, and you are sure to have a slow trip across at this season.

Just then a young man, with the softest black eyes and a clear pale complexion, came into the office. The agent, Mr. Harmon, introduced him to me as Mr. Fuhrmann, the purser of the Oceanic, the ship on which I would eventually travel to Japan and America. The young man took my hand in a firm, strong clasp, and his soft black eyes gave me such a look of sympathy that it only needed his kind tone to cheer me into a happier state.

"I went down to the Oriental to meet you; Mr. Harmon thought it was better. We want to take good care of you now that you are in our charge, but, unfortunately, I missed you. I returned to the hotel, and as they knew nothing about you there I came here, fearing that you were lost."

"I have found kind friends everywhere," I said, with a slight motion towards the doctor, who was speechless over the ill-luck that had befallen me. "I am sorry to have been so much trouble to you."

"Trouble! You are with your own people now, and we are only too happy if we can be of service," he said kindly. "You must not mind about the possibility of some one getting around the world in less time than you may do it. You have had the worst connections it is possible to make, and everybody knows the idea originated with you, and that others are merely trying to steal the work of your brain, so, whether you get in before or later, people will give you the credit of having originated the idea."

"I promised my editor that I would go around the world in seventy-five days, and if I accomplish that I shall be satisfied," I stiffly explained.

"I am not racing with anyone. I would not race. If someone else wants to do the trip in less time, that is their concern. If they take it upon themselves to race *against* me, it is their lookout that they succeed. I am not racing. I promised to do the trip in seventy-five days, and I will do it; although had I been permitted to make the trip when I first proposed it over a year ago, I should then have done it in sixty days."

We returned to the hotel, where a room had been secured for me, after arranging the transfer of my luggage and the monkey from the Oriental to the Oceanic. I met a number of people after tiffin, who were interested in my trip, and were ready and anxious to do anything they could to contribute to my pleasure during my enforced stay.

Having but the one dress I refused to attend any dinners or receptions that were proposed in my honor. During the afternoon the wife of a prominent Hong Kong gentleman waited upon me to place herself and her home at my disposal. She was anxious that I should make her home mine during my stay, but I told her I could not think of accepting her kindness, because I would wish to be out most of the time, and could not make my hours conform to the hours of the house, and still feel free to go, come and stay, as I pleased. Despite her pleadings I assured her I was not on pleasure bent, but business, and I considered it my duty to refrain from social pleasures, devoting myself to things that lay more in the line of work.

I had dinner on the Oriental. As I bade the captain and his officers farewell, remembering their kindness to me, I had a wild desire to cling to them, knowing that with the morning light the Oriental would sail, and I would be once again alone in strange lands with strange people.

That evening the purser of the Oceanic, another acquaintance and I were carried in chairs up a winding road, arched with green trees, on which the leaves hung motionless and still in the silent night.

Our lazy voices, as occasionally we spoke softly to each other, and the steady, monotonous slap-slap-slap of the bare-feet of our carriers made the only break in the slumbering stillness. All earth seemed to have gone to rest. Silently we went along, now getting, by dim gas lamps at garden gates, glimpses of comfortable homes in all their Eastern splendor, and then, for a moment emerging from beneath the over-lapping arch of verdant trees, we would get a faint glimmer of the quivering stars and cloudless heavens. The ascent was made at last. We were above the city, lying dark and quiet, but no nearer the glorious starlit sky. A little rush through a wide gate in a high wall, a sudden blindness in a road banked and roofed by foliage, a quick lowering to the ground at the foot of wide steps that led to an open door through which a welcoming light shed its soft, warm rays upon us and we had reached our journey's end.

Inside, where a cordial welcome awaited us, was a bright wood fire before which I longed to curl up on a rug and be left alone to dream—dream. But there were friends instead of dreams, and realities in the shape of a splendid dinner. A table, graced with a profusion of tropical blossoms—a man, handsomer than an ideal hero, at its head—a fine menu, guests, handsome, witty and just enough in number to suit my ideas, were the items of what made up an ideal evening.

It is said people do not grow old in Hong Kong. Their youthful looks bear ample testimony to the statement. I asked the reason why, and they said it is because they are compelled to invent amusements for themselves, and by inventing they find, not time to grow *blasé*, but youth and happiness.

The theatre in Hong Kong knows few professional troupes, but the amateur actors in the English colony leave little to be desired in the way of splendid entertainments. The very best people in the town take part, and I believe they all furnish their own stage costumes. The regiments stationed there turn out very creditable actors in the persons of the young officers. I went one night to see "Ali Baba and the Forty Thieves" as given by the Amateur Dramatic Club of Hong Kong. It was a new version of the old story filled with local hits arranged for the club by a military captain; the music was by the band-master of the Argyll and Sutherland Highlanders. The beautiful and artistic scenery was designed and executed by two army men, as were the lime-light effects. Spectators came to the theatre in their chairs instead of carriages.

Inside, the scene was bewitching. A rustling of soft gowns, the odor of flowers, the fluttering of fans, the sounds of soft, happy whispering, a maze of lovely women in evening gowns mingling with handsome men in the regulation evening dress—what could be prettier? If American women would only ape the English in going bonnetless to the theatres, we would forgive their little aping in other respects, and call it even. Upon the arrival of the Governor the band played "God Save the Queen," during which the audience stood. Happily, they made it short. The play was pleasantly presented, the actors filling their roles most creditably, especially the one taking the part of Alley Sloper.

Afterwards, the sight of handsomely dressed women stepping into their chairs, the daintily-colored Chinese lanterns, hanging fore and aft, marking the course the carriers took in the darkness, was very oriental and affective. It is a luxury to have a carriage, of course, but there is something even more luxurious in the thought of owning a chair and carriers. A fine chair with silver mounted poles and silk hangings can be bought, I should judge, for a little more than twenty dollars. Some women keep four and eight carriers; they are so cheap that one can afford to retain a number. Every member of a well established household in Hong Kong has his or her own private chair. Many men prefer a coverless willow chair with swinging step, while many women have chairs that close entirely, so they can be carried along the streets secure against the gaze of the public. Convenient pockets, umbrella stands and places for parcels are found in all well-appointed chairs.

At every port I touched I found so many bachelors, men of position, means and good appearance, that I naturally began to wonder why women do not flock that way. It was all very well some years ago to say, "Go West, young man;" but I would say, "Girls, go East!" There are bachelors enough and to spare! And a most happy time do these bachelors have in the East. They are handsome, jolly and good natured. They have their own fine homes with no one but the servants to look after them. Think of it, and let me whisper, "Girls, go East!"

The second day after my arrival, Captain Smith, of the Oceanic, called upon me. I expected to see a hard-faced old man; so, when I went into the drawing-room and a youthful, good-looking man, with the softest blue eyes that seemed to have caught a tinge of the ocean's blue on a bright day, smiled down at me, I imagine I must have looked very stupid indeed. I looked at the smooth, youthful face, with its light-brown moustache, and I felt inclined to laugh at the long iron-gray beard my imagination had put upon the Captain of the Oceanic. I caught a laughing gleam of the bluest of blue eyes, and I thought of imaginary stern ones, and had to smother another insane desire to laugh. I looked at the tall, slender, shapely body, and recalled the imaginary short legs, holding upright a wide circumference under an ample waistcoat, and I laughed audibly.

"You were so different to what I imagined you would be," I said afterwards, when we talked over our first meeting.

"And I could not believe you were the right girl, you were so unlike what I had been led to believe," he said, with a laugh, in a burst of confidence. "I was told that you were an old maid with a dreadful temper. Such horrible things were said about you that I was hoping you would miss our ship. I said if you did come I supposed you would expect to sit at my table, but I would arrange so you should be placed elsewhere."

The Captain took me out to see "Happy Valley" that day before we separated. In jinrickshas we rode by the parade and cricket grounds where some lively games are played, the city hall, and the solid, unornamented barracks; along smooth, tree-lined roads, out to where the mountains make a nest of one level, green space. This level has been converted into a race-course. The judges' stand was an ordinary, commonplace race-course stand, but the stands erected by and for private families, were built of palms and were more pleasing because they were out of the usual.

During the month of February races are held here annually. They last three days, and during that period everybody stops work, rich and poor alike flocking to the race-course. They race with native-bred Mongolian ponies, having no horses, and the racing is pronounced most exciting and interesting.

"Happy Valley" lines the hillside. There are congregated the graveyards of all the different sects and nationalities in Hong Kong. The Fire Worshipers lie in ground joining the Presbyterians, the Episcopalians, the Methodists and the Catholics, and Mahommedans are just as close by. That those of different faiths should consent to place their dead together in this lovely tropical valley is enough to give it the name of Happy Valley, if its beauty did not do as much. In my estimation it rivals in beauty the public gardens, and visitors use it as a park. One wanders along the walks looking at the beautiful shrubs and flowers, never heeding that they are in the valley of death, so thoroughly is it robbed of all that is horrible about graveyards. We rode back to town through the crowded districts, where the natives huddle together in all their filth. It is said that over 100,000 people live within a certain district in Hong Kong not exceeding one-half square mile, and they furthermore positively affirm, that sixteen hundred people live in the space of an acre. This is a sample of the manner in which the Chinese huddle together. They remind me of a crowd of ants on a lump of sugar. An effort is being made in Hong Kong to compel owners to build differently, so as to make the huddling and packing impossible, for the filth that goes with it invariably breeds disease.

Queen's road is interesting to all visitors. In it is the Hong Kong Club, where the bachelors are to be found, the post office, and greater than all, the Chinese shops. The shops are not large, but the walls are lined with black-wood cabinets, and one feels a little thrill of pleasure at the sight of the gold, the silver, ivory carvings, exquisite fans, painted scrolls and the odor of the lovely sandal-wood boxes, coming faintly to the visitor, creates a feeling of greed. One wants them all—everything.

The Chinese merchants cordially show their goods, or follow as one strolls around, never urging one to buy, but cunningly bringing to the front the most beautiful and expensive part of their stock.

"Chin chin," which means "good day," "good bye," "good night," "How are you?" or anything one may take from it, is the greeting of Chinamen. They all speak mongrel English, called "pidgin" or "pigeon" English. It is impossible to make them understand pure English, consequently Europeans, even housekeepers, use pidgin English when addressing the servants. The servants are men, with the exception of the nurses, and possibly the cooks. To the uninitiated it sounds absurd to hear men and women addressing servants and merchants in the same idiotic language with which fond parents usually cuddle their offspring; but even more laughable is it to hear men swear in "pigeon English," at an unkind or unruly servant. Picture a man with an expression of frenzied rage upon his countenance, saying:

"Go to hellee, savey?"

Pidgin or pigeon, is applied to everything. One will hear people say: " Hab got pigeon," which means they have business to look after; or if a Chinaman is requested to do some work which he thinks is the duty of another, he will say: "No belongee boy pigeon."

While strolling about the Chinese localities, seeing shops more worthy a visit, being more truly Chinese, I came upon an eating house, from which a conglomeration of strange odors strolled out and down the road. Built around a table in the middle of the room, was a circular bench. The diners perched on this bench like chickens on a fence, not letting their feet touch the floor, or hang over, nor "hunkering" down, nor squatting crossed-legged like a Turk or tailor, but sitting down with their knees drawn up until knees and chin met; they held large bowls against their chins, pushing the rice energetically with their chop-sticks into their mouths. Cup after cup of tea is consumed, not only at meals, but at all hours during the day. The cup is quite small and saucerless, and the tea is always drank minus sugar and cream.

Professional writers, found in nooks and recesses of prominent thoroughfares, are interesting personalities. Besides writing letters for people they tell fortunes, and their patrons never go away without having their fates foretold. I noticed when paying for articles, merchants invariably weigh the money. It is also customary for merchants to put their private stamp upon silver dollars as an assurance of its legality and worth. Much silver is beaten into such strange shapes by this queer practice that at first I was afraid to accept it in change.

I saw a marriage procession in Hong Kong. A large band of musicians, who succeeded in making themselves heard, were followed by coolies carrying curious looking objects in blue and gilt, which, I was told, represent mythical and historical scenes. A number of very elegant Chinese lanterns and gorgeous looking banners were also carried along. I was told that in such processions they carry roast pig to the temples of the josses, but it is afterwards very sensibly carried off by the participants.

It would be a hopeless thing for a man to go to Hong Kong in search of employment. The banking and shipping houses, controlled by Europeans, certainly employ numbers of men, but they are brought from England under three and five years' contracts. When a vacancy occurs from a death, or a transfer, the business house immediately consults its representatives in London, where another man signs an agreement, and comes out to Hong Kong to work.

One day I went up to Victoria Peak, named in honor of the Queen. It is said to be 1,800 feet high, the highest point on the island. An elevated tramway is built from the town to Victoria Gap, 1,100 feet above the sea. It was opened in 1887. Before that time people were carried up in sedans.

The first year after its completion 148,344 passengers were carried up the mountain side. The fare is thirty cents up and fifteen cents down. During the summer months Hong Kong is so hot that those who are in a position to do so seek the mountain top, where a breeze lives all the year round. Level places for buildings are obtained by blasting, and every brick, stone, and bit of household furniture is carried by coolies from the town up to the height of 1,600 feet.

At the Gap we secured sedan chairs, and were carried to the Hotel Craigiburn, which is managed by a colored man. The hotel—Oriental in style—is very liberally patronized by the citizens of Hong Kong, as well as visitors. After the proprietor had shown us over the hotel and given us a dinner that could not be surpassed we were carried to Victoria Peak. It required three men to a chair ascending the peak. At the Umbrella Seat, merely a bench with a peaked roof, everybody stops long enough to allow the coolies to rest, then we continue on our way, passing sight-seers and nurses with children. After a while they stop again, and we travel on foot to the signal station.

The view is superb. The bay, in a breastwork of mountains, lies calm and serene, dotted with hundreds of ships that seem like tiny toys. The palatial white houses come half way up the mountain side, beginning at the edge of the glassy bay. Every house we notice has a tennis-court blasted out of the mountain side. They say that after night the view from the peak is unsurpassed. One seems to be suspended between two heavens. Every one of the several thousand boats and sampans carries a light after dark. This, with the lights on the roads and in the houses, seems to be a sky more filled with stars than the one above.

Early one morning a gentleman, who was the proud possessor of a team of ponies, the finest in Hong Kong, called at the hotel to take me for a drive. In a low, easy phaeton behind the spirited ponies that seem like playthings in their smallness but giants in their strength, we whirled along through the town and were soon on the road edging the bay. We had a good view of the beautiful dry dock on the other side, which is constructed entirely of granite and is said to be of such size that it can take in the largest vessels afloat. I thought there were other things more interesting, so I refused to go over to it.

During our drive we visited two quaint and dirty temples. One was a plain little affair with a gaudy altar. The stone steps leading to it were filled with beggars of all sizes, shapes, diseases and conditions of filth. They were so repulsive that instead of appealing to one's sympathy they only succeed in arousing one's disgust.

At another temple, near by a public laundry where the washers stood in a shallow stream slapping the clothes on flat stones, was a quaint temple hewed, cave-like, in the side of an enormous rock. A selvage of rock formed the altar, and to that humble but picturesque temple Chinese women flock to pray for sons to be born unto them that they may have some one to support them in their old age.

After seeing everything of interest in Hong Kong I decided to go to a real Simon-pure Chinese city. I knew we were trying to keep the Chinamen out of America, so I decided to see all of them I could while in their land. Pay them a farewell visit, as it were! So, on Christmas eve, I started for the city of Canton.

XIII

Christmas in Canton

The O. and O. agent escorted me to the ship Powan, on which I was to travel to Canton. He gave me in charge of Captain Grogan, the Powan's commander, an American, who has lived for years in China. A very bashful man he was, but a most kindly, pleasant one. I never saw a fatter man, or a man so comically fattened. A wild inclination to laugh crept over me every time I caught a glimpse of his roly-poly body, his round red face embedded, as it were, in the fat of his shoulders and breast. The thoughts of how sensitive I am concerning remarks about my personal appearance, in a measure subdued my impulse to laugh. I have always said to critics, who mercilessly write about the shape of my chin, or the cut of my nose, or the size of my mouth, and such personal attributes that can no more be changed than death can be escaped:

"Criticise the style of my hat or my gown, I can change them, but spare my nose, it was born on me."

Remembering this, and how nonsensical it is to blame or criticise people for what they are powerless to change, I pocketed my merriment, letting a kindly feeling of sympathy take its place.

Soon after we left, night descended. I went on deck where everything was buried in darkness. Softly and steadily the boat swam on, the only sound—and the most refreshing and restful sound in the world—was the lapping of the water.

To sit on a quiet deck, to have a star-lit sky the only light above or about, to hear the water kissing the prow of the ship, is, to me, paradise. They can talk of the companionship of men, the splendor of the sun, the softness of moonlight, the beauty of music, but give me a willow chair on a quiet deck, the world with its worries and noise and prejudices lost in distance, the glare of the sun, the cold light of the moon blotted out by the dense blackness of night. Let me rest rocked gently by the rolling sea, in a nest of velvety darkness, my only light the soft twinkling of the myriads of stars in the quiet sky above; my music, the round of the kissing waters, cooling the brain and easing the pulse; my companionship, dreaming my own dreams. Give me that and I have happiness in its perfection.

But away with dreams. This is a work-a-day world and I am racing Time around it. After dinner, when the boat anchored, waiting for the tide which was to carry us safely over the bar, I went below to see the Chinese passengers. They were gambling, smoking opium, sleeping, cooking, eating, reading and talking, all huddled together on one deck, which was in one large room, not divided into cabins. They carry their own beds, a bit of matting, and their own food, little else than rice and tea.

Before daybreak we anchored at Canton. The Chinamen went ashore the moment we landed, but the other passengers remained for breakfast.

While we were having breakfast, the guide whom the captain had secured for us, came on board and quietly supervised the luncheon we were to take with us. A very clever fellow was that guide, Ah Cum. The first thing he said to us was "A Merry Christmas!" and as it had even slipped our minds, I know we all appreciated the polite thoughtfulness of our Chinese guide. Ah Cum told me later that he had been educated in an American mission located in Canton, but he assured me, with great earnestness, that English was all he learned. He would have none of the Christian religion. Ah Cum's son was also educated in an American mission, and, like his father, has put his learning to good account. Besides being paid as guide, Ah Cum collects a percentage from merchants for all the goods bought by tourists. Of course the tourists pay higher prices than they would otherwise, and Ah Cum sees they visit no shops where he is not paid his little fee.

Ah Cum is more comely in features than most Mongolians, his nose being more shapely and his eyes less slit-like than those of most of his race. He had on his feet beaded black shoes with white soles. His navy-blue trousers, or tights, more properly speaking, were tied around the ankle and fitted very tight over most of the leg. Over this he wore a blue, stiffly starched shirt-shaped garment, which reached his heels, while over this he wore a short padded and quilted silk jacket, somewhat similar to a smoking jacket. His long, coal-black queue, finished with a tassel of black silk, touched his heels, and on the spot where the queue began rested a round black turban.

Ah Cum had chairs ready for us. His chair was a neat arrangement in black, black silk hangings, tassels, fringe and black wood-poles finished with brass knobs. Once in it, he closed it, and was hidden from the gaze of the public. Our plain willow chairs had ordinary covers, which, to my mind, rather interfered with sightseeing. We had three coolies to each chair. Those with us were bare-footed, with tousled pig-tail and navy-blue shirts and trousers, much the worse for wear both in cleanliness and quality. Ah Cum's coolies wore white linen garments, gayly trimmed with broad bands of red cloth, looking very much like a circus clown's costume.

Ah Cum led the way, our coolies following. For a time I was only conscious of a confused mass of black faces and long pig tails, though shortly I became accustomed to it, and was able to distinguish different objects along the crowded thoroughfare; could note the different stands and the curious looks of the people. We were carried along dark and dirty narrow ways, in and about fish stands, whence odors drifted, filling me with disgust, until we crossed a bridge which spanned a dark and sluggish stream.

This little island, guarded at every entrance, is Shameen, or Sandy Face, the land set aside for the habitation of Europeans. An unchangeable law prohibits Celestials from crossing into this sacred precinct, because of the hatred they cherish for Europeans. Shameen is green and picturesque, with handsome houses of Oriental design, and grand shade trees, and wide, velvety green roads, broken only by a single path, made by the bare feet of the chair-carriers.

Here, for the first time since leaving New York, I saw the stars and stripes. It was floating over the gateway to the American Consulate. It is a strange fact that the further one goes from home the more loyal one becomes. I felt I was a long ways off from my own dear land; it was Christmas day, and I had seen many different flags since last I gazed upon our own. The moment I saw it floating there in the soft, lazy breeze I took off my cap and said: "That is the most beautiful flag in the world, and I am ready to whip anyone who says it isn't."

No one said a word. Everybody was afraid! I saw an Englishman in the party glance furtively towards the Union Jack, which was floating over the English Consulate, but in a hesitating manner, as if he feared to let me see.

Consul Seymour received our little party with a cheery welcome. He was anxious that we should partake of his hospitality, but we assured him our limited time only gave us a moment to pay our respects, and then we must be off again.

Mr. Seymour was an editor before he went to China with his wife and only daughter, to be consul. Since then he has conceived a hobby for embroideries and carved ivories, which he is able to ride to the top of his bent in Canton. When tourists go there he always knows some place where he can guide them to bargains. Mr. Seymour is a most pleasant, agreeable man, and a general favorite. It is to be hoped that he will long have a residence in Shameen, where he reflects credit upon the American Consulate.

What a different picture Canton presents to Shameen. They say there are millions of people in Canton. The streets, many of which are roughly paved with stone, seem little over a yard in width. The shops, with their gayly colored and handsomely carved signs, are all open, as if the whole end facing the street had been blown out. In the rear of every shop is an altar, gay in color and often expensive in adornment. As we were carried along the roads we could see not only the usually rich and enticing wares, but the sellers and buyers. Every shop has a book-keeper's desk near the entrance. The book-keepers all wear tortoise-shell rimmed glasses of an enormous size, which lend them a look of tremendous wisdom. I was inclined to think the glasses were a mark of office, for I never saw a man employed in clerical work without them.

I was warned not to be surprised if the Chinamen should stone me while I was in Canton. I was told that Chinese women usually spat in the faces of female tourists when the opportunity offered. However, I had no trouble. The Chinese are not pleasant appearing people; they usually look as if life had given them nothing but trouble; but as we were carried along the men in the stores would rush out to look at me. They did not take any interest in the men with me, but gazed at me as if I was something new. They showed no sign of animosity, but the few women I met looked as curiously at me, and less kindly.

The thing that seemed to interest the people most about me were my gloves. Sometimes they would make bold enough to touch them, and they would always gaze upon them with looks of wonder.

The streets are so narrow that I thought at first I was being carried through the aisles of some great market. It is impossible to see the sky, owing to the signs and other decorations, and the compactness of the buildings; and with the open shops, just like stands in a market, except that they are not even cut off from the passing crowd by a counter, the delusion is a very natural one. When Ah Cum told me that I was not in a market-house, but in the streets of the city of Canton, my astonishment knew no limit. Sometimes our little train would meet another train of chairs, and then we would stop for a moment and there would be great yelling and fussing until we had safely passed, the way being too narrow for both trains to move at once in safety.

Coolie number two of my chair was a source of great discomfort to me all the day. He had a strap spanning the poles by which he upheld his share of the chair. This band, or strap, crossed his shoulders, touching the neck just where the prominent bone is. The skin was worn white and hard-looking from the rubbing of the band; but still it worried me, and I watched all the day expecting to see it blister. His long pig-tail was twisted around his head, so I had an unobstructed view of the spot. He was not an easy traveler, this coolie, there being as much difference in the gait of carriers as there is in the gait of horses. Many times he shifted the strap, much to my misery, and then he would turn and, by motions, convey to me that I was sitting more to one side than to the other.

As a result, I made such an effort to sit straight and not to move that when we alighted at the shops I would be cramped almost into a paralytic state. Before the day was over I had a sick headache, all from thinking too much about the comfort of the Chinamen.

A disagreeable thing about the coolies is that they grunt like pigs when carrying one. I can't say whether the grunt has any special significance to them or not, but they will grunt one after the other along the train, and it is anything but pleasant.

I was very anxious to see the execution ground, so we were carried there. We went in through a gate where a stand erected for gambling was surrounded by a crowd of filthy people. Some few idle ones left it to saunter lazily after us. The place is very unlike what one would naturally suppose it to be. At first sight it looked like a crooked back alley in a country town. There were several rows of half dried pottery. A woman, who was moulding in a shed at one side, stopped her work to gossip about us with another female who had been arranging the pottery in rows. The place is probably seventy-five feet long by twenty-five wide at the front, and narrowing down at the other end. I noticed the ground in one place was very red, and when I asked Ah Cum about it he said indifferently, as he kicked the red-colored earth with his white-souled shoe:

"It's blood. Eleven men were beheaded here yesterday."

He added that it was an ordinary thing for ten to twenty criminals to be executed at one time. The average number per annum is something like 400. The guide also told us that in one year, 1855, over 50,000 rebels were beheaded in this narrow alley.

While he was talking I noticed some roughly fashioned wooden crosses leaned up against the high stone wall, and supposing they were used in some manner for religious purposes before and during the executions, I asked Ah Cum about them. A shiver waggled down my spinal cord when he answered:

"When women are condemned to death in China they are bound to wooden crosses and cut to pieces."

"Men are beheaded with one stroke unless they are the worst kind of criminals," the guide added, "then they are given the death of a woman to make it the more discreditable. They tie them to the crosses and strangle or cut them to pieces. When they are cut to bits, it is done so deftly that they are entirely dismembered and disemboweled before they are dead. Would you like to see some heads?"

I thought that Chinese guide could tell as large stories as any other guides; and who can equal a guide for highly-colored and exaggerated tales? So I said coldly:

"Certainly; bring on your heads!"

I tipped a man, as he told me, who, with the clay of the pottery on his hands, went to some barrels which stood near to the wooden crosses, put in his hand and pulled out a head!

Those barrels are filled with lime, and as the criminals are beheaded their heads are thrown into the barrels, and when the barrels become full they empty them out and get a fresh supply. If a man of wealth is condemned to death in China he can, with little effort, buy a substitute. Chinamen are very indifferent about death; it seems to have no terror for them.

I went to the jail and was surprised to see all the doors open. The doors were rather narrow, and when I got inside and saw all the prisoners with thick, heavy boards fastened about their necks, I no longer felt surprised at the doors being unbarred. There was no need of locking them.

I went to the court, a large, square, stone-paved building. In a small room off one side I was presented to some judges who were lounging about smoking opium! In still another room I met others playing fan tan! At the entrance I found a large gambling establishment! They took me into a room to see the instruments of punishment. Split bamboo to whip with, thumb screws, pulleys on which people are hanged by their thumbs, and such pleasant things. While I was there they brought in two men who had been caught stealing. The thieves were chained with their knees meeting their chins, and in that distressing position were carried in baskets suspended on a pole between two coolies. The judges explained to me that as these offenders had been caught in the very act of taking what belonged not to them, their hands would be spread upon flat stones and with smaller stones every bone in their hands would be broken. Afterwards they would be sent to the hospital to be cured. Prisoners dying in jail are always beheaded before burial.

An American who has lived many years near Canton told me there is a small bridge spanning a stream in the city where it is customary to hang criminals in a fine wire hammock, first removing all their clothing. A number of sharp knives are laid at the end of the bridge, and every one crossing while the man is there is compelled to take a knife and give a slash to the wire-imprisoned wretch. As I saw none of this myself, I only give these stories as they were given to me.

They tell me bamboo punishment (I cannot now recall the name they gave it) is not as uncommon in China as one would naturally suppose from its extreme brutality. For some crimes offenders are pinioned in standing position with their legs astride, fastened to stakes in the earth. This is done directly above a bamboo sprout. To realize this punishment in all its dreadfulness it is necessary to give a little explanation of the bamboo. A bamboo sprout looks not unlike the delicious asparagus, but is of a hardness and strength not equaled by iron. When it starts to come up, nothing can stop its progress. It is so hard that it will go through anything on its way up; let that anything be asphalt or what it will, the bamboo goes through it as readily as though the obstruction didn't exist. The bamboo grows with marvelous rapidity straight up into the air for thirty days, and then it stops. When its growth is finished it throws off a shell-like bark, its branches slowly unfolding and falling into place. They are covered with a soft airy foliage finer than the leafage of a willow. From a distance a bamboo forest is a most beautiful thing, exquisitely soft and fine in appearance, but adamant is not harder in reality. As I have said, nothing can stop a bamboo sprout when it intends to come up. Nothing ever equaled the rapidity of its growth, it being affirmed that it can really be seen growing! In the thirty days that it grows it may reach a height of seventy-five feet.

Picture then a convict pinioned above a bamboo sprout and in such a position that he cannot get away from it. It starts on its upward course never caring for what is in its way; on it goes through the man who stands there dying, dying, worse than by inches, conscious for a while, then fever mercifully kills knowledge, and at last, after days of suffering, his head drops forward, and he is dead. But that is not any worse than tying a man in the boiling sun to a stake, covering him with quick-lime and giving him nothing but water to quench hunger and thirst. He holds out and out, for it means life, but at last he takes the water that is always within his reach. He drinks, he perspires, and the lime begins to eat. They also have a habit of suspending a criminal by his arms, twisting them back of him. As long as a man keeps his muscles tense he can live, but the moment he relaxes and falls, it ruptures blood vessels and his life floats out on a crimson stream. The unfortunate is always suspended in a public place, where magistrates watch so that no one may release him. Friends of the condemned flock around the man of authority, bargaining for the man's life; if they can pay the price extorted by him the man is taken down and set free; if not, he merely hangs until the muscles give out and he drops to death. They also have a way of burying the whole of criminals except their heads. The eyelids are fastened back so that they cannot close them, and so facing the sun they are left to die. Sticking bamboo splints under the finger nails and then setting fire to them is another happy way of punishing wrongdoers.

I had no idea what I was to see when we mounted the filthy stone steps leading to the Temple of Horrors. I concluded it most be an exhibition of human monstrosities. The steps were filled with dirty Mongolians of all sizes, ages, shapes and afflictions. When they heard our steps, those who could see and walk, rushed up to us, crying for alms, and those who were blind and powerless raised their voices the louder because they could not move. Inside, a filthy stone court was crowded with a mass of humanity. There were lepers, peddlers, monstrosities, fortune tellers, gamblers, quacks, dentists with strings of horrid teeth, and even pastry cooks! It is said the Chinese worship here occasionally and consult idols. In little, dirty cells were dirty figures, representing the punishment of the Buddhists' hell. They were being whipped, ground to death, boiled in oil, beheaded, put under red hot bells, being sawed in twain, and undergoing similar agreeable things.

Canton is noted for its many curious and interesting temples. There are over eight hundred temples in the city. The most interesting one I saw during my flying trip was the Temple of the Five Hundred Gods. While there the guide asked me if I was superstitious, and upon my answering in the affirmative, he said he would show me how to try my luck. Placing some joss sticks in a copper jar before the luck-god, he took from the table two pieces of wood, worn smooth and dirty from frequent use, which, placed together, were not unlike a pear in shape. With this wood—he called it the "luck pigeon"—held with the flat sides together, he made circling motions over the smouldering joss sticks, once, twice, thrice, and dropped the luck pigeon to the floor. He explained if one side of the luck pigeon turned up and the other turned down it meant good luck, while if they both fell in the same position it meant bad luck. When he dropped it they both turned the one way, and he knew he would have bad luck.

I took the luck pigeon then, and I was so superstitious that my arm trembled and my heart beat in little palpitating jumps as I made the motions over the burning joss sticks. I dropped the wood to the floor, and one piece turned one way and one the other, and I was perfectly happy. I knew I was going to have good luck.

I saw the Examination Hall, where there are accommodations for the simultaneous examination of 11,616 celestial students, all male. We went to the entrance-gate through a dirty park-like space where a few stunted trees grew feebly and a number of thin, black pigs rooted energetically. Dirty children in large numbers followed us, demanding alms in boisterous tones, and a few women who, by the aid of canes, were hobbling about on their cramped small feet, stopped to look after us with grins of curiosity and amusement. The open space is the principal entrance, then we go through a small gate called the gate of Equity, and later still another called the Dragon gate, which leads into the great avenue. A most strange and curious sight this avenue gives. An open space with a tower on the end known as the watch tower, has a god of literature in the second story. On each side of the open green space are rows of whitewashed buildings, not unlike railway cattle yards in appearance. In these ranges of cells, cells that measure 5-½ by 3-⅔ feet, 11,616 pig-tailed students undergo their written examination. On the sides facing the avenue are Chinese inscriptions showing what study is examined in that range. In each cell is a board to sit on, and one a little higher for a desk. This roughly improvised desk must be slid out to allow the student to enter or depart unless he crawls under or jumps over. The same texts are given to all at daylight, and very often when essays are not finished at night the students are kept over night in their cells. The Hall is about 1,380 feet long by 650 feet wide, and is really a strangely interesting place well worth a visit. It is said the examinations are very severe, and from the large number of candidates examined, sometimes only one hundred and fifty will be passed. The place in which the essays are examined is called the Hall of Auspicious Stars, and the Chinese inscription over the avenue translated reads, "The opening heavens circulate literature."

I had a great curiosity to see the leper village, which is commonly supposed to contain hundreds of Chinese lepers. The village consists of numbers of bamboo huts, and the lepers present a sight appalling in its squalor and filth. Ah Cum told us to smoke cigarettes while in the village so that the frightful odors would be less perceptible. He set the example by lighting one, and we all followed his lead. The lepers were simply ghastly in their misery. There are men, women and children of all ages and conditions. The few filthy rags with which they endeavored to hide their nakedness presented no shape of any garment or any color, so dirty and ragged were they. On the ground floors of the bamboo huts were little else than a few old rags, dried grass and things of that kind. Furniture there was none. It is useless to attempt a description of the loathsome appearance of the lepers. Many were featureless, some were blind, some had lost fingers, others a foot, some a leg, but all were equally dirty, disgusting and miserable. Those able to work cultivate a really prosperous-looking garden, which is near their village. Ah Cum assured me they sold their vegetables in the city market! I felt glad to know we had brought our luncheon from the ship. Those lepers able to walk spend the day in Canton begging, but are always compelled to sleep in their village, still I could not help wondering what was the benefit of a leper village if the lepers are allowed to mingle with the other people. On my return to the city I met several lepers begging in the market. The sight of them among the food was enough to make me vow never to eat anything in Canton. The lepers are also permitted to marry, and a surprising number of diseased children are brought into a cursed and unhappy existence.

As we left the leper city I was conscious of an inward feeling of emptiness. It was Christmas day, and I thought with regret of dinner at home, although one of the men in the party said it was about midnight in New York. The guide said there was a building near by which he wanted to show us and then we would eat our luncheon. Once within a high wall we came upon a pretty scene. There was a mournful sheet of water undisturbed by a breath of wind. In the background the branches of low, overhanging trees kissed the still water just where stood some long-legged storks, made so familiar to us by pictures on Chinese fans.

Ah Cum led us to a room which was shut off from the court by a large carved gate. Inside were hard wood chairs and tables. While eating I heard chanting to the weird, plaintive sound of a tom-tom and a shrill pipe. When I had less appetite and more curiosity, I asked Ah Cum where we were, and he replied: "in the Temple of the Dead."

And in the Temple of the Dead I was eating my Christmas luncheon. But that did not interfere with the luncheon. Before we had finished a number of Chinaman crowded around the gate and looked curiously at me. They held up several children, well clad, cleanly children, to see me. Thinking to be agreeable, I went forward to shake hands with them, but they kicked and screamed, and getting down, rushed back in great fright, which amused us intensely. Their companions succeeded after awhile in quieting them and they were persuaded to take my hand. The ice once broken, they became so interested in me, my gloves, my bracelets and my dress, that I soon regretted my friendliness in the outset.

It is customary at the death of a person to build a bonfire after night, and cast into the fire household articles, such as money boxes, ladies' dressing cases, etc., composed of gilt paper, the priests meanwhile playing upon shrill pipes. They claim the devil which inhabits all bodies leaves the body to save the property of the dead, and once they play him out he can never re-enter, so souls are saved.

I climbed high and dirty stone steps to the water-clock, which, they say, is over five hundred years old, and has never run down or been repaired. In little niches in the stone walls were small gods, before them the smouldering joss sticks. The water-clock consists of four copper jars, about the size of wooden pails, placed on steps, one above the other. Each one has a spout from which comes a steady drop-drop. In the last and bottom jar is an indicator, very much like a foot rule, which rises with the water, showing the hour. On a blackboard hanging outside, they mark the time for the benefit of the town people. The upper jar is filled once every twenty-fear hours, and that is all the attention the clock requires.

On our return to the Powan I found some beautiful presents from Consul Seymour and the cards of a number of Europeans who had called to see me. Suffering from a sick-headache, I went to my cabin and shortly we were on our way to Hong Kong, my visit to Canton on Christmas day being of the past.

XIV

To the Land of the Mikado

Shortly after my return to Hong Kong I sailed for Japan on the Oceanic. A number of friends, who had contributed so much towards my pleasure and comfort during my stay in British China, came to the ship to say farewell, and most regretfully did I take leave of them. Captain Smith took us into his cabin, where we all touched glasses and wished one another success, happiness and the other good things of this earth. The last moment having come, the final good-bye being said, we parted, and I was started on my way to the land of the Mikado.

The Oceanic, on which I traveled from Hong Kong to San Francisco, has quite a history. When it was designed and launched twenty years ago by Mr. Harland, of Belfast, it startled the shipping world. The designer was the first to introduce improvements for the comfort of passengers, such as the saloon amidships, avoiding the noise of the engines and especially the racing of the screw in rough weather. Before that time ships were gloomy and somber in appearance and constructed without a thought of the happiness of passengers. Mr. Harland, in the Oceanic, was the first to provide a promenade deck and to give the saloon and staterooms a light and cheerful appearance. In fact, the Oceanic was such a new departure that it aroused the jealousy of other ship companies, and was actually condemned by them as unseaworthy. It is said that so great was the outcry against the ship that sailors and firemen were given extra prices to induce them to make the first trip.

Instead of being the predicted failure, the Oceanic proved a great success. She became the greyhound of the Atlantic, afterwards being transferred to the Pacific in 1875. She is the favorite ship of the O. and O. line, making her voyages with speed and regularity. She retains a look of positive newness and seems to grow younger with years. In November, 1889, she made the fastest trip on record between Yokohama and San Francisco. No expense is spared to make this ship comfortable for the passengers. The catering would be hard to excel by even a first-class hotel. Passengers are accorded every liberty, and the officers do their utmost to make their guests feel at home, so that in the

Orient the Oceanic is the favorite ship, and people wait for months so as to travel on her.

When I first went to the ship the monkey had been transferred from the Oriental. Meeting the stewardess I asked how the monkey was, to which she replied dryly:

"We have met."

She had her arm bandaged from the wrist to the shoulder!

"What did you do?" I asked in consternation.

"I did nothing but scream; the monkey did the rest!" she replied.

I spent New Year's eve between Hong Kong and Yokohama. The day had been so warm that we wore no wraps. In the forepart of the evening the passengers sat together in Social Hall talking, telling stories and laughing at them. The captain owned an organette which he brought into the hall, and he and the doctor took turns at grinding out the music. Later in the evening we went to the dining-hall where the purser had punch and champagne and oysters for us, a rare treat which he had prepared in America just for this occasion.

What children we all become on board a ship! After oysters we were up to all sorts of childish tricks. As we sat around the table the doctor gave us each a word to say, such as Ish! Ash! Osh! Then when we were sure of our word, it coming in rotation around the circle, he told us to shout the words in unison when he gave the signal. We did, and it made one great big sneeze—the most gigantic and absurd sneeze I ever heard in my life. Afterwards a jolly man from Yokohama, whose wife was equally jolly and lively-spirited, taught us a song consisting of one line to a melody quite simple and catching.

"Sweetly sings the donkey when he goes to grass, Sweetly sings the donkey when he goes to grass, Ec-ho! Ec-ho! Ec-ho!"

When eight bells rang we rose and sang Auld Lang Syne with glasses in hand, and on the last echo of the good old song toasted the death of the old year and the birth of the new. We shook hands around, each wishing the other a happy New Year. 1889 was ended, and 1890 with its pleasures and pains began. Shortly after, the women passengers retired. I went to sleep lulled by the sounds of familiar negro melodies sung by the men in the smoking-room beneath my cabin.

XV

ONE HUNDRED AND TWENTY
HOURS IN JAPAN

After seeing Hong Kong with its wharfs crowded with dirty boats manned by still dirtier people, and its streets packed with a filthy crowd, Yokohama has a cleaned-up Sunday appearance. Travelers are taken from the ships, which anchor some distance out in the bay, to the land in small steam launches. The first-class hotels in the different ports have their individual launches, but like American hotel omnibuses, while being run by the hotel to assist in procuring patrons, the traveler pays for them just the same.

An import as well as an export duty is charged in Japan, but we passed the custom inspectors unmolested. I found the Japanese jinricksha men a gratifying improvement upon those I seen from Ceylon to China. They presented no sight of filthy rags, nor naked bodies, nor smell of grease. Clad in neat navy-blue garments, their little pudgy legs encased in unwrinkled tights, the upper half of their bodies in short jackets with wide flowing sleeves; their clean, good-natured faces, peeping from beneath comical mushroom-shaped hats; their blue-black, wiry locks cropped just above the nape of the neck, they offered a striking contrast to the jinricksha men of other countries. Their crests were embroidered upon the back and sleeves of their top garment as are the crests of every man, woman and child in Japan.

Rain the night previous had left the streets muddy and the air cool and crisp, but the sun creeping through the mistiness of early morning, fell upon us with most gratifying warmth. Wrapping our knees with rugs the 'ricksha men started off in a lively trot to the Pacific Mail and O. and O. Companies' office, where I met discourteous people for the first time since I left the P. & O. "Victoria." And these were Americans, too. The most generous excuse that can be offered for them is that they have held their positions so long that they feel they are masters, instead of a steamship company's servants. A man going into the office to buy a ticket to America, was answered in the following manner by one of the head men:

"You'll have to come back later if you want a ticket. I'm going to lunch now."

I stayed at the Grand Hotel while in Japan. It is a large building, with long verandas, wide halls and airy rooms, commanding an exquisite view of the lake in front. Barring an enormous and monotonous collection of rats, the Grand would be considered a good hotel even in America. The food is splendid and the service excellent. The "Japs," noiseless, swift, anxious to please, stand at the head of all the servants I encountered from New York to New York; and then they look so neat in their blue tights and white linen jackets.

I always have an inclination to laugh when I look at the Japanese men in their native dress. Their legs are small and their trousers are skin tight. The upper garment, with its great wide sleeves, is as loose as the lower is tight. When they finish their "get up" by placing their dish-pan shaped hat upon their heads, the wonder grows how such small legs can carry it all! Stick two straws in one end of a potato, a mushroom in the other, set it up on the straws and you have a Japanese in outline. Talk about French heels! The Japanese sandal is a small board elevated on two pieces of thin wood fully five inches in height. They make the people look exactly as if they were on stilts. These queer shoes are fastened to the foot by a single strap running between toes number one and two, the wearer when walking necessarily maintaining a sliding instead of an up and down movement, in order to keep the shoe on.

On a cold day one would imagine the Japanese were a nation of armless people. They fold their arms up in their long, loose sleeves. A Japanese woman's sleeves are to her what a boy's pockets are to him. Her cards, money, combs, hair pins, ornaments and rice paper are carried in her sleeves. Her rice paper is her handkerchief, and she notes with horror and disgust that after using we return our handkerchiefs to our pockets. I think the Japanese women carry everything in their sleeves, even their hearts. Not that they are fickle—none are more true, more devoted, more loyal, more constant, than Japanese women—but they are so guileless and artless that almost any one, if opportunity offers, can pick at their trusting hearts.

If I loved and married, I would say to my mate: "Come, I know where Eden is," and like Edwin Arnold, desert the land of my birth for Japan, the land of love—beauty—poetry—cleanliness. I somehow always connected Japan and its people with China and its people, believing the one no improvement on the other. I could not have made a greater mistake. Japan is beautiful. Its women are charmingly sweet. I know little about the men except that they do not go far as we judge manly beauty, being undersized, dark, and far from prepossessing. They have the reputation of being extremely clever, so I do not speak of them as a whole, only of those I came in contact with. I saw one, a giant in frame, a god in features; but he was a public wrestler.

The Japanese are the direct opposite to the Chinese. The Japanese are the cleanliest people on earth, the Chinese are the filthiest; the Japanese are always happy and cheerful, the Chinese are always grumpy and morose; the Japanese are the most graceful of people, the Chinese the most awkward; the Japanese have few vices, the Chinese have all the vices in the world; in short, the Japanese are the most delightful of people, the Chinese the most disagreeable.

The majority of the Europeans live on the bluff in low white bungalows, with great rooms and breezy verandas, built in the hearts of Oriental gardens, where one can have an unsurpassed view of the Mississippi bay, or can play tennis or cricket, or loll in hammocks, guarded from public gaze by luxurious green hedges. The Japanese homes form a great contrast to the bungalows. They are daintily small, like play houses indeed, built of a thin shingle-like board, fine in texture. Chimneys and fireplaces are unknown. The first wall is set back, allowing the upper floor and side walls to extend over the lower flooring, making it a portico built in instead of on the house. Light window frames, with their minute openings covered with fine rice paper instead of glass, are the doors and windows in one. They do not swing open and shut as do our doors, nor do they move up and down like our windows, but slide like rolling doors. They form the partitions of the houses inside and can be removed at any time, throwing the floor into one room.

They have two very pretty customs in Japan. The one is decorating their houses in honor of the new year, and the other celebrating the blossoming of the cherry trees. Bamboo saplings covered with light airy foliage and pinioned so as to incline towards the middle of the street, where meeting they form an arch, make very effective decorations. Rice trimmings mixed with sea-weed, orange, lobster and ferns are hung over every door to insure a plentiful year, while as sentinels on either side are large tubs, in which are three thick bamboo stalks, with small evergreen trees for background.

In the cool of the evening we went to a house that had been specially engaged to see the dancing, or *geisha*, girls. At the door we saw all the wooden shoes of the household, and we were asked to take off our shoes before entering, a proceeding rather disliked by some of the party, who refused absolutely to do as requested. We effected a compromise, however, by putting cloth slippers over our shoes. The second floor had been converted into one room, with nothing in it except the matting covering the floor and a Japanese screen here and there. We sat upon the floor, for chairs there are none in Japan, but the exquisite matting is padded until it is as soft as velvet. It was laughable to see us trying to sit down, and yet more so to see us endeavor to find a posture of ease for our limbs. We were about as graceful as an elephant dancing. A smiling woman in a black kimono set several round and square charcoal boxes containing burning charcoal before us. These are the only Japanese stove. Afterwards she brought a tray containing a number of long-stemmed pipes—Japanese women smoke constantly—a pot of tea and several small cups.

Impatiently I awaited the *geisha* girls. In the tiny maidens glided at last, clad in exquisite trailing, angel-sleeved kimonos. The girls bow gracefully, bending down until their heads touch their knees, then kneeling before us murmur gently a greeting which sounds like "Koinbanwa!" drawing in their breath with a long, hissing suction, which is a token of great honor. The musicians sat down on the floor and began an alarming din upon *samisens*, drums and gongs, singing meanwhile through their pretty noses. If the noses were not so pretty I am sure the music would be unbearable to one who has ever heard a chest note. The *geisha* girls stand posed with open fan in hand above their heads, ready to begin the dance. They are very short with the slenderest of slender waists. Their soft and tender eyes are made blacker by painted lashes and brows; their midnight hair, stiffened with a gummy wash, is most wonderfully dressed in large coils and ornamented with gold and silver flowers and gilt paper pom-pons. The younger the girl the more gay is her hair. Their kimonos, of the most exquisite material, trail all around them, and are loosely held together at the waist with an obi-sash; their long flowing sleeves fall back, showing their dimpled arms and baby hands. Upon their tiny feet they wear cunning white linen socks cut with a place for the great toe. When they go out they wear wooden sandals. The Japanese are the only women I ever saw who could rouge and powder and be not repulsive, but the more charming because of it. They powder their faces and have a way of reddening their under lip just at the tip that gives them a most tempting look. The lips look like two luxurious cherries. The musicians begin a long chanting strain, and these bits of beauty begin the dance. With a grace, simply enchanting, they twirl their little fans, sway their dainty bodies in a hundred different poses, each one more intoxicating than the other, all the while looking so childish and shy, with an innocent smile lurking about their lips, dimpling their soft cheeks, and their black eyes twinkling with the pleasure of the dance. After the dance the *geisha* girls made friends with me, examining, with surprised delight, my dress, my bracelets, my rings, my boots—to them the most wonderful and extraordinary things,—my hair, my gloves, indeed they missed very little, and they approved of all. They said I was very sweet, and urged me to come again, and in honor of the custom of my land—the Japanese never kiss—they pressed their soft, pouting lips to mine in parting.

Japanese women know nothing whatever of bonnets, and may they never! On rainy days they tie white scarfs over their wonderful hair-dressing, but at other times they waddle bareheaded, with fan and umbrella, along the streets on their wooden clogs. They have absolutely no furniture. Their bed is a piece of matting, their pillows, narrow blocks of wood, probably six inches in length, two wide and six high. They rest the back of the neck on the velvet covered top, so their wonderful hair remains dressed for weeks at a time. Their tea and pipe always stand beside them, so they can partake of their comforts the last thing before sleep and the first thing after.

A Japanese reporter from Tokyo came to interview me, his newspaper having translated and published the story of my visit to Jules Verne. Carefully he read the questions which he wished to ask me. They were written at intervals on long rolls of foolscap, the space to be filled in as I answered. I thought it ridiculous until I returned and became an interviewee. Then I concluded it would be humane for us to adopt the Japanese system of interviewing.

I went to Kamakura to see the great bronze god, the image of Buddha, familiarly called Diabutsu. It stands in a verdant valley at the foot of two mountains. It was built in 1250 by Ono Goroyemon, a famous bronze caster, and is fifty feet in height; it is sitting Japanese style, ninety-eight feet being its waist circumference; the face is eight feet long, the eye is four feet, the ear six feet six and one-half inches, the nose three feet eight and one-half inches, the mouth is three feet two and one-half inches, the diameter of the lap is thirty-six feet, and the circumference of the thumb is over three feet. I had my photograph taken sitting on its thumb with two friends, one of whom offered $50,000 for the god. Years ago at the feast of the god sacrifices were made to Diabutsu. Quite frequently the hollow interior would be heated to a white heat, and hundreds of victims were cast into the seething furnace in honor of the god. It is different now, sacrifices being not the custom, and the hollow interior is harmlessly fitted up with tiny altars and a ladder stairway by which visitors can climb up into Diabutsu's eye, and from that height view the surrounding lovely country. We also visited a very pretty temple near by, saw a famous fan tree and a lotus-pond, and spent some time at a most delightful tea-house, where two little "Jap" girls served us with tea and sweets. I also spent one day at Tokio, where I saw the Mikado's Japanese and European castles, which are enclosed by a fifty foot stone wall and three wide moats. The people in Tokio are trying to ape the style of the Europeans. I saw several men in native costume riding bicycles. Their roads are superb. There is a street car line in Tokio, a novelty in the East, and carriages of all descriptions. The European clothing sent to Japan is at least ready-made, if not second hand. One woman I saw was considered very stylish. The bodice of a European dress she wore had been cut to fit a slender, tapering waist. The Japanese never saw a corset and their waists are enormous. The woman was able to fasten one button at the neck, and from that point the bodice was permitted to spread. She was considered very swell. At dinner one night I saw a "Jap" woman in a low cut evening dress, with nothing but white socks on her feet.

It would fill a large book if I attempted to describe all I saw during my stay in Japan. Going to the great Shiba temple, I saw a forest of superb trees. At the carved gate leading to the temple were hundreds of stone and bronze lanterns, which alone were worth a fortune. On either side of the gate were gigantic carved images of ferocious aspect. They were covered with wads of chewed paper. When I remarked that the school children must make very free with the images, a gentleman explained that the Japanese believed if they chewed paper and threw it at these gods and it stuck their prayers would be answered, if not, their prayers would pass unheeded. A great many prayers must have been answered. At another gate I saw the most disreputable looking god. It had no nose. The Japanese believe if they have a pain or ache and they rub their hands over the face of that god, and then where the pain is located, they will straightway be cured. I can't say whether it cured them or not, but I know they rubbed away the nose of the god.

The Japanese are very progressive people. They cling to their religion and their modes of life, which in many ways are superior to ours, but they readily adopt any trade or habit that is an improvement upon their own. Finding the European male attire more serviceable than their native dress for some trades they promptly adopted it. The women tested the European dress, and finding it barbarously uncomfortable and inartistic went back to their exquisite kimonos, retaining the use of European underwear, which they found more healthful and comfortable than the utter absence of it, to which they had been accustomed. The best proof of the comfort of kimonos lies in the fact that the European residents have adopted them entirely for indoor wear. Only their long subjection to fashion prevents their wearing them in public. Japanese patriotism should serve as a model for us careless Americans. No foreigner can go to Japan and monopolize a trade. It is true that a little while ago they were totally ignorant of modern conveniences. They knew nothing of railroads, or street cars, or engines, or electric lighting. They were too clever though to waste their wits in efforts to rediscover inventions known to other nations, but they had to have them. Straightway they sent to other countries for men who understood the secret of such things, and at fabulous prices and under contracts of three, five and occasionally ten years duration, brought them to their land. They were set to work, the work they had been hired to do, and with them toiled steadily and watchfully the cleverest of Japanese. When the contract is up it is no longer necessary to fill the coffers of a foreigner. The employé was released, and their own man, fully qualified for the work, stepped into the position. And so in this way they command all business in their country.

Kimonos are made in three parts, each part an inch or so longer than the other. I saw a kimono a Japanese woman bought for the holidays. It was a suit, gray silk crepe, with pink peach blossoms dotting it here and there. The whole was lined with the softest pink silk, and the hem, which trails, was thickly padded with a delicate perfume sachet. The underclothing was of the flimsiest white silk. The whole thing cost sixty dollars, a dollar and a half of which paid for the making. Japanese clothing is sewed with what we call a basting stitch, but it is as durable as it could be if sewed with the smallest of stitches. Japanese women have mirrors in which they view their numerous charms. Their mirrors are round, highly polished steel plates, and they know nothing whatever of glass mirrors. All the women carry silk card cases in their long sleeves, in which are their own diminutive cards.

English is taught in the Japan schools and so is gracefulness. The girls are taught graceful movements, how to receive, entertain and part with visitors, how to serve tea and sweets gracefully, and the proper and graceful way to use chopsticks. It is a pretty sight to see a lovely woman use chopsticks. At a tea-house or at an ordinary dinner a long paper laid at one's place contains a pair of chopsticks, probably twelve inches in length, but no thicker than the thinner size of lead pencils. The sticks are usually whittled in one piece and split only half apart to prove that they have never been used. Every one breaks the sticks apart before eating, and after the meal they are destroyed.

An American resident of Japan told me of his going to see a cremation. The Japanese graveyard is a strange affair, with headstones set close together, leaving the space for the graves less than the size of a baby's grave in America. As soon as the breath has left a body it is undressed and doubled up, head to feet, and is made to go in a very small bamboo box built in imitation of a Japanese house. This house may cost a great deal of money. It is carried along the streets on two poles to the place where it is to be cremated where it is given in charge of the cremator, and the friends go back to their homes until the following day, when they return for the ashes, which are generally placed in an urn and buried. The American, of whom I spoke, made arrangements with a cremator, and, accompanied by a friend, walked to the place in the country and waited out of sight until the mourners had vanished before they dared to draw near enough to see the cremation. They had walked quite a distance, dinnerless, and said, naively, that the odor was like that of veal, and it made him ravenously hungry.

A small hole about three feet long is made in the earth and in it the fire is built. When it was the proper heat the box was set over it, and in an instant it was consumed. The body released from its doubled position straightened out. The lower half being over the fire was soon cremated, excepting the feet and knee joints. The man in charge carefully pulled the upper part of the body over the fire, and with the same large fork put the half-consumed feet and knee-joints under the arms. In less than an hour all that remained of the body was a few ashes in the bottom of the pit. While the cremator was explaining it all to the gentleman he repeatedly filled his little pipe and lit it with the fire from the burning body. At his urgent request the gentleman consented to take tea with him when his task was done. They entered his neat little home while he jumped into a boiling bath in the open garden, from which he emerged later as red as a lobster. Meanwhile his charming and pretty daughters were dispensing the hospitalities of their home to their guests, and the father, desirous of enjoying their society, came and stood in the doorway, talking to them and watching them eat while he wiped his naked body with a towel!

The prettiest sight in Japan, I think, is the native streets in the afternoons. Men, women and children turn out to play shuttle-cock and fly kites. Can you imagine what an enchanting sight it is to see pretty women with cherry lips, black bright eyes, ornamented, glistening hair, exquisitely graceful gowns, tidy white-stockinged feet thrust into wooden sandals, dimpled cheeks, dimpled arms, dimpled baby hands, lovely, innocent, artless, happy, playing shuttlecock in the streets of Yokohama?

Japanese children are unlike any other children I ever saw at play. They always look happy and never seem to quarrel or cry. Little Japanese girls, elevated on wooden sandals and with babies almost as large as themselves tied on their backs, play shuttle-cock with an abandon that is terrifying until one grows confident of the fact that they move with as much agility as they could if their little backs were free from nursemaid burdens. Japanese babies are such comical little fellows. They wear such wonderfully padded clothing that they are as shapeless as a feather pillow. Others may think, as I did, that the funny little shaven spots on their heads was a queer style of ornamentation, but it is not. I am assured the spots are shaven to keep their baby heads cool.

The Japanese are not only pretty and artistic but most obliging. A friend of mine who guided us in Japan had a Kodak, and whenever we came upon an interesting group he was always taking snap shots. No one objected, and especially were the children pleasant about being photographed. When he placed them in position, or asked them to stand as they were, they would pose like little drum-majors until he gave them permission to move.

The only regret of my trip, and one I can never cease to deplore, was that in my hasty departure I forgot to take a Kodak. On every ship and at every port I met others—and envied them—with Kodaks. They could photograph everything that pleased them; the light in those lands is excellent, and many were the pleasant mementos of their acquaintances and themselves they carried home on their plates. I met a German who was spending two years going around the world and he carried two Kodaks, a large and a small size, and his collection of photographs was the most interesting I ever saw. At the different ports he had professional photographers develop his plates.

The Japanese thoughtfully reserve a trade for their blind. They are all taught massage bathing, and none but the blind are allowed to follow this calling. These people go through the streets uttering to a plaintive melody these words:

"I'll give you a bath from head to toe for two cents."

At Uyeno park, where they point out a tree planted by General Grant when on his tour around the world, I saw a most amusing monkey which belonged to the very interesting menagerie. It was very large and had a scarlet face and gray fur. It was chained to the fence, and when one of the young men in our party went up and talked to him the monkey looked very sagacious and wise. In the little crowd that gathered around, quite out of the monkey's reach, was a young Jap, who, in a spirit of mischief, tossed a pebble at the red-faced mystery, who turned with a grieved and inquiring air to my friend.

"Go for him," my friend responded, sympathetically, to the look, and the monkey turned and with its utmost strength endeavored to free itself so it could obey the bidding. The Jap made his escape and the monkey quieted down, looking expressively at the place where the Jap had stood and then at my friend for approval, which he obtained. The keeper gave the monkey its dinner, which consisted of two large boiled sweet potatoes. My friend broke one in two and the monkey greedily ate the inside, placing the remainder with the other potato on the fence between his feet. Suddenly he looked up, and as quick as a flash he flung, with his entire force, which was something terrific, the remaining potato at the head of some one in the crowd. There was some loud screaming and a scattering, but the potato missing all heads, went crashing with such force against a board fence that every particle of it remained sticking there in one shapeless splotch. The Jap who had tossed the pebble at the monkey, and so earned his enmity, quietly shrunk away with a whitened face. He had returned unnoticed by all except the monkey, who tried to revenge himself with the potato. I admired the monkey's cleverness so much that I would have tried to buy him if I had not already owned one.

In Yokohama, I went to Hundred Steps, at the top of which lives a Japanese belle, Oyuchisan, who is the theme for artist and poet, and the admiration of tourists. One of the pleasant events of my stay was the luncheon given for me on the Omaha, the American war vessel lying at Yokohama. I took several drives, enjoying the novelty of having a Japanese running by the horses' heads all the while. I ate rice and eel. I visited the curio shops, one of which is built in imitation of a Japanese house, and was charmed with the exquisite art I saw there; in short, I found nothing but what delighted the finer senses while in Japan.

XVI

Across the Pacific

I t was a bright sunny morning when I left Yokohama. A number of new friends in launches escorted me to the Oceanic, and when we hoisted anchor the steam launches blew loud blasts upon their whistles in farewell to me, and the band upon the Omaha played "Home, Sweet Home," "Hail Columbia," and "The Girl I Left Behind Me," in my honor; and I waved my handkerchief so long after they were out of sight that my arms were sore for days. My feverish eagerness to be off again on my race around the world was strongly mingled with regret at leaving such charming friends and such a lovely land.

Everything promised well for a pleasant and rapid voyage. Anticipating this, Chief-engineer Allen caused to be written over the engines and throughout the engine room, this date and couplet:

> "For Nellie Bly,
> We'll win or die.
> January 20, 1890."

It was their motto and was all very sweet to me. The runs were marvelous until the third day out, and then a storm came upon us. They tried to cheer me, saying it would only last that day, but the next day found it worse, and it continued, never abating a moment; head winds, head sea, wild rolling, frightful pitching, until I fretfully waited for noon when I would slip off to the dining-room to see the run, hoping that it would have gained a few miles on the day before, and always being disappointed. And they were all so good to me! Bless them for it! If possible, they suffered more over the prospect of my failure than I did.

"If I fail, I will never return to New York," I would say despondently; "I would rather go in dead and successful than alive and behind time."

"Don't talk that way, child," Chief Allen would plead, "I would do anything for you in my power. I have worked the engines as they never were worked before; I have sworn at this storm until I have no words left; I have even prayed—I haven't prayed before for years—but I prayed that this storm may pass over and that we may get you in on time."

"I know that I am not a sinner," I laughed hysterically. "Day and night my plea has been, 'Be merciful to me a sinner,' and as the mercy has not been forthcoming, the natural conclusion is that I'm not a sinner. It's hopeless, it's hopeless!"

"Don't think so," the purser would beg; "don't be so disheartened; why, child, if by jumping overboard I could bring you happiness and success, I should do so in a moment."

"Never mind, little girl, you're all right," the jolly, happy-hearted captain would laugh. "I've bet every cent I have in the bank that you'll get in before you are due. Just take my word for it, you'll be in New York at least three days ahead of time."

"Why do you try to cheat me? You know we are way behind time now," I urged, longing to be still farther cheated into fresh hope, to which the doctor would say, dryly:

"Look here, Nellie Bly, if you don't stop talking so I'll make you take some pills for your liver."

"You mean wretch, you know I can't help being blue. It's head sea, and head winds, and low runs—not liver!"

And then I would laugh, and so would they; and Mr. Allen, who had been pleading for me to "smile just once, give them but one glimpse of my old, jolly smile," would go away content. This is but a repetition of the way in which I was coaxed out of my unhappiness every day, by those great-hearted, strong, tender men.

At last a rumor became current that there was a Jonah on board the ship. It was thought over and talked over and, much to my dismay, I was told that the sailors said monkeys were Jonahs. Monkeys brought bad weather to ships, and as long as the monkey was on board we would have storms. Some one asked if I would consent to the monkey being thrown overboard. A little struggle between superstition and a feeling of justice for the monkey followed. Chief Allen, when I spoke to him on the subject, told me not to do it. He said the monkey had just gotten outside of a hundred weight of cement, and had washed it down with a quart of lamp oil, and he, for one, did not want to interfere with the monkey's happiness and digestion! Just then some one told me that ministers were Jonahs; they always brought bad weather to ships. We had two ministers on board! So I said quietly, if the ministers were thrown overboard I'd say nothing about the monkey. Thus the monkey's life was saved.

Mr. Allen had a boy, Walter, who was very clever at tricks. One day Walter said he would show that he could lift a bottle merely by placing his open hand to the side of the bottle. He put everybody out of the cabin, as he said if they remained in it broke the influence. They watched intently through the open door as he rolled up his sleeve and rubbed his arm downward, quite vigorously, as if trying to get all the blood in his hand. Catching the wrist with the other hand, as if to hold all the blood there, he placed his open hand to the side of (the) bottle and, much to the amazement of his audience, the bottle went up with his hand. When urged to tell how to do the wonderful trick, he said:

"It's all very easy; all you do is to rub your arm, that's just for show; then you lay hold of your wrist just as if you wanted to keep all the blood in your hand; you keep one finger free—no one notices that— and you take the neck of the bottle between the hand and the finger, and the bottle goes up with the hand. See?"

One evening, when the ship was rolling frightfully, everybody was gathered in the dining-hall; an Englishman urged Walter to do some tricks, but Walter did not want to be bothered then, so he said: "Yes, sir; in a moment, sir," and went on putting the things upon the table. He had put down the mustard pot, the salt cellar and various things, and was wiping a plate. As he went to put the plate down the ship gave a great roll, the plate knocked against the mustard pot and the mustard flew all over the Englishman, much to the horror of the others. Sitting up stiffly, the mustard dotting him from head to knees, he said sternly:

"Walter! What is this?"

"That, sir, is the first trick," Walter replied softly, and he glided silently and swiftly off to the regions of the cook.

But Walter was caught one day. A sailor told him that he could hide an egg on him so no one would be able to find it. Walter had his doubts, but he willingly gave the sailor a test. The egg was hidden and a man called in to find it. He searched Walter all over without once coming upon the egg. The sailor suggested another trial to which Walter, now an interested and firm believer in the sailor's ability, gladly consented. The sailor opened Walter's shirt and placed the egg next to the skin in the region of his heart, carefully buttoning the shirt afterwards. The man was called in, he went up to Walter and hit him a resounding smack where Sullivan hit Kilrain. He found the egg and so did Walter!

Japanese "boys" serve in the dining-hall on the Oceanic, but the sailors are Chinese. They chant in a musical manner when hoisting sails. It sounds as if they say "Ah-Oh-Eh-Oh! Ah-Oh-Eh-Ah-Oh!"

The "boys" shake the tablecloths into a plate. They put a plate in the tablecloth which two of them shake once or twice and then slide the plate to the floor. The plate will be seen to have gathered all the crumbs.

One Chinaman and one Japanese traveled first-class coming over. The Chinaman was confined to his cabin with sea-sickness all the time, so we saw very little of him. The Japanese wore European dress and endeavored to ape the manners of the Europeans. Evidently he thought it the custom to use tooth-picks. It is—with some people. After every meal he used a tooth-pick so that the whole table might see, as if wishing to show he was civilized! Then after a great amount of gorging he always placed the tooth-pick pen-like behind his ear where it stayed until the next meal.

But even with low runs our trip was bound to come to an end. One night it was announced that the next day we would be in San Francisco. I felt a feverish excitement, and many were the speculations as to whether there would be a snow blockade to hinder my trip across the Continent. A hopefulness that had not known me for many days came back, when in rushed the purser, his face a snow-white, crying:

"My God, the bill of health was left behind in Yokohama."

"Well—well—what does that mean?" I demanded, fearing some misfortune, I knew not what.

"It means," he said, dropping nerveless into a chair, "that no one will be permitted to land until the next ship arrives from Japan. That will be two weeks."

The thought of being held two weeks in sight of San Francisco, in sight of New York almost, and the goal for which I had been striving and powerless to move, was maddening.

"I would cut my throat, for I could not live and endure it," I said quietly, and that spurred him on to make another search, which resulted in finding the report safely lodged in the doctor's desk.

Later came a scare about a small-pox case on board, but it proved to be only a rumor, and early in the morning the revenue officers came aboard bringing the newspapers. I read of the impassable snow blockade which for a week had put a stop to all railroad traffic, and my despair knew no bounds. While the Oceanic was waiting for the quarantine doctor, some men came out on a tug to take me ashore. There was no time for farewells. The monkey was taken on the tug with me, and my baggage, which had increased by gifts from friends, was thrown after me. Just as the tug steamed off the quarantine doctor called to me that he had forgotten to examine my tongue, and I could not land until he did. I stuck it out, he called out "all right;" the others laugh, I wave farewell, and in another moment I was parted from my good friends on the Oceanic.

XVII

ACROSS THE CONTINENT

I only remember my trip across the continent as one maze of happy greetings, happy wishes, congratulating telegrams, fruit, flowers, loud cheers, wild hurrahs, rapid hand-shaking and a beautiful car filled with fragrant flowers attached to a swift engine that was tearing like mad through flower-dotted valley and over snow-tipped mountain, on—on—on! It was glorious! A ride worthy a queen. They say no man or woman in America ever received ovations like those given me during my flying trip across the continent. The Americans turned out to do honor to an American girl who had been the first to make a record of a flying trip around the world, and I rejoiced with them that it was an American girl who had done it. It seemed as if my greatest success was the personal interest of every one who greeted me. They were all so kind and as anxious that I should finish the trip in time as if their personal reputations were at stake. The special train had been waiting for my arrival in readiness to start the moment I boarded it. The Deputy Collector of the port of San Francisco, the Inspector of Customs, the Quarantine Officer and the Superintendent of the O. and O. steamers sat up all the night preceding my arrival, so there should be no delay in my transfer from the Oceanic to the special train. Nor were they the only ones to wait for me. One poor little newspaper woman did not see bed that night so anxious was she for an interview which she did not get. I was so entirely ignorant about what was to be done with me on landing, that I thought I was someone's guest until I was many miles away from San Francisco. Had I known in advance the special train was mine, every newspaper man and woman who cared to should have been my guest.

My train consisted of one handsome sleeping-car, the San Lorenzo, and the engine, The Queen, was one of the fastest on the Southern Pacific.

"What time do you want to reach New York, Miss Bly?" Mr. Bissell, General Passenger Agent of the Atlantic and Pacific system, asked me.

"Not later than Saturday evening," I said, never thinking they could get me there in that time.

"Very well, we will put you there on time," he said quietly, and I rested satisfied that he would keep his word.

It did not seem long after we left Oakland Mole until we reached the great San Joaquin valley, a level green plain through which the railroad track ran for probably three hundred miles as straight as a sunbeam. The road-bed was so perfect that though we were traveling a mile a minute the car was as easy as if it were traveling over a bed of velvet.

At Merced, our second stop, I saw a great crowd of people dressed in their best Sunday clothes gathered about the station. I supposed they were having a picnic and made some such remark, to be told in reply that the people had come there to see me. Amazed at this information I got up, in answer to calls for me, and went out on the back platform. A loud cheer, which almost frightened me to death, greeted my appearance and the band began to play "By Nellie's Blue Eyes." A large tray of fruit and candy and nuts, the tribute of a dear little newsboy, was passed to me, for which I was more grateful than had it been the gift of a king.

We started on again, and the three of us on the train had nothing to do but admire the beautiful country through which we were passing as swiftly as cloud along the sky, to read, or count telegraph poles, or pamper and pet the monkey. I felt little inclination to do anything but to sit quietly and rest, bodily and mentally. There was nothing left for me to do now. I could hurry nothing, I could change nothing; I could only sit and wait until the train landed me at the end of my journey. I enjoyed the rapid motion of the train so much that I dreaded to think of the end. At Fresno, the next station, the town turned out to do me honor, and I was the happy recipient of exquisite fruits, wines and flowers, all the product of Fresno County, California.

The men who spoke to me were interested in my sun-burnt nose, the delays I had experienced, the number of miles I had traveled. The women wanted to examine my one dress in which I had traveled around, the cloak and cap I had worn, were anxious to know what was in the bag, and all about the monkey.

While we were doing some fine running the first day, I heard the whistle blow wildly, and then I felt the train strike something. Brakes were put on, and we went out to see what had occurred. It was hailing just then, and we saw two men coming up the track. The conductor came back to tell us that we had struck a hand-car, and pointed to a piece of twisted iron and a bit of splintered board—all that remained of it—

laying alongside. When the men came up, one remarked, with a mingled expression of wonder and disgust upon his face:

"Well, you ARE running like h—!"

"Thank you; I am glad to hear it," I said, and then we all laughed. I inquired if they had been hurt; they assured me not, and good humor being restored all around, we said good-bye, the engineer pulled the lever, and we were off again. At one station where we stopped there was a large crowd, and when I appeared on the platform, one yell went up from them. There was one man on the outskirts of the crowd who shouted:

"Nellie Bly, I must get up close to you!"

The crowd evidently felt as much curiosity as I did about the man's object, for they made a way and he came up to the platform.

"Nellie Bly, you must touch my hand," he said, excitedly. Anything to please the man. I reached over and touched his hand, and then he shouted:

"Now you will be successful. I have in my hand the left hind foot of a rabbit!"

Well, I don't know anything about the left hind foot of a rabbit, but when I knew that my train had run safely across a bridge which was held in place only by jack-screws, and which fell the moment we were across; and when I heard that in another place the engine had just switched off from us when it lost a wheel, then I thought of the left hind foot of a rabbit, and wondered if there was anything in it.

One place, where a large crowd greeted me, a man on the limits of it yelled:

"Did you ride on an elephant, Nellie?" and when I said I had not, he dropped his head and went away. At another place the policemen fought to keep the crowd back; everybody was wanting to shake hands with me, but at last one officer was shoved aside, and the other seeing the fate of his comrade, turned to me, saying: "I guess I'll give up and take a shake," and while reaching for my hand was swept on with the crowd. I leaned over the platform and shook hands with both hands at every station, and when the train pulled out crowds would run after, grabbing for my hands as long as they could. My arms ached for almost a month afterwards, but I did not mind the ache if by such little acts I could give pleasure to my own people, whom I was so glad to be among once more.

"Come out here and we'll elect you governor," a Kansas man said, and I believe they would have done it, if the splendid welcomes they gave me are any criterion. Telegrams addressed merely to "Nellie Bly, Nellie Bly's Train," came from all parts of the country filled with words of cheer and praise at all hours of the day and night. I could not mention one place that was kinder than another. Over ten thousand people greeted me at Topeka. The mayor of Dodge City presented me, in behalf of the citizens, with resolutions of praise. I was very anxious to go to Kansas City, but we only went to the station outside of the limits, in order to save thirty minutes. At Hutchinson a large crowd and the Ringgold Cornet Band greeted me, and at another place the mayor assured me that the band had been brought down, but they forgot to play. They merely shouted like the rest, forgetting in the excitement all about their music.

I was up until four o'clock, talking first with a little newspaper girl from Kearney, Nebraska, who had traveled six hundred miles to meet and interview me, and later dictating an account of my trip to a stenographer, who was sea-sick from the motion of the train. I had probably slept two hours when the porter called me, saying we would soon be in Chicago. I dressed myself leisurely and drank the last drop of coffee there was left on our train, for we had been liberally entertaining everybody who cared to travel any distance with us. I was surprised, on opening the door of my state-room, to see the car quite filled with good-looking men. They were newspaper men, members of the Chicago Press Club, I found a moment later, who had come out to Joliet to meet me and to escort me to their city. Mr. Cornelius Gardener, the vice-president of the club, in the absence of the president, took charge of our little party. Before we were in I had answered all their questions, and we joked about my sun-burnt nose and discussed the merits of my one dress, the cleverness of the monkey, and I was feeling happy and at home and wishing I could stay all day in Chicago.

Carriages were waiting to take us to the rooms of the Press Club. I went there in a coupe with Vice-President Gardener who said, in a published narration of my visit afterwards, that he was strongly tempted to steal me, which clever idea so amused me that had the case been reversed, I know I should have acted on it, much to the confusion of a waiting public in New York. In the beautiful rooms of the Press Club I met the president, Stanley Waterloo, and a number of clever newspaper men. I had not been expected in Chicago until noon, and the club had arranged an informal reception for me, and when they were notified of my speedy trip and consequently earlier arrival, it was too late to notify the members. After a most delightfully informal reception I was escorted to Kinsley's, where the club had a breakfast prepared. And then I learned that, owing to some misunderstanding, none of the men had had anything to eat since the night before. After breakfast the members of the Press Club, acting as my escort, took me to visit the Chicago Board of Trade. When we went in, the pandemonium which seems to reign during business hours was at its height. My escorts took me to the gallery, and just as we got there a man raised his arm to yell something to the roaring crowd, when he saw me, and yelled instead:

"There's Nellie Bly!"

In one instant the crowd that had been yelling like mad became so silent that a pin could have been heard fall to the floor. Every face, bright and eager, was turned up towards us, instantly every hat came off, and then a burst of applause resounded through the immense hall. People can say what they please about Chicago, but I do not believe that anywhere else in the United States a woman can get a greeting which will equal that given by the Chicago Board of Trade. The applause was followed by cheer after cheer and cries of "Speech!" but I took off my little cap and shook my head at them, which only served to increase their cheers.

Shortly afterwards the Press Club escorted me to the Pennsylvania Station, where I reluctantly bade them good-bye, unable to thank them heartily enough for the royal manner in which they had treated a little sun-burnt stranger.

Now I was on a regular train which seemed to creep, so noticeable was the difference in the speed of traveling. Instead of a fine sleeping-car at my disposal, I had but a state-room, and my space was so limited that floral and fruit offerings had to be left behind. In Chicago, a cable which afforded me much pleasure reached me, having missed me at San Francisco.

"Mr. Verne wishes the following message to be handed to Nellie Bly the moment she touches American soil: M. and Mme. Jules Verne address their sincere felicitations to Miss Nellie Bly at the moment when that intrepid young lady sets foot on the soil of America."

The train was rather poorly appointed, and it was necessary for us to get off for our meals. When we stopped at Logansport for dinner, I being the last in the car, was the last to get off. When I reached the platform a young man, whom I never saw before or since, sprang upon the other platform, and waving his hat, shouted:

"Hurrah for Nellie Bly!"

The crowd clapped hands and cheered, and after making way for me to pass to the dining-room, pressed forward and cheered again, crowding to the windows at last to watch me eat. When I sat down, several dishes were put before me bearing the inscription, "Success, Nellie Bly."

It was after dark when we reached Columbus, where the depot was packed with men and women waiting for me. A delegation of railroad men waited upon me and presented me with beautiful flowers and candy, as did a number of private people. I did not go to bed until after we had passed Pittsburgh, and only got up in the morning in time to greet the thousands of good people who welcomed me at Harrisburg, where the Harrisburg Wheelman's Club sent a floral offering in remembrance of my being a wheelman. A number of Philadelphia newspaper men joined me there, and at Lancaster I received an enthusiastic reception.

Almost before I knew it I was at Philadelphia, and all too soon to please me, for my trip was so pleasant I dreaded the finish of it. A number of newspaper men and a few friends joined me at Philadelphia to escort me to New York. Speech-making was the order from Philadelphia on to Jersey City. I was told when we were almost home to jump to the platform the moment the train stopped at Jersey City, for that made my time around the world. The station was packed with thousands of people, and the moment I landed on the platform, one yell went up from them, and the cannons at the Battery and Fort Greene boomed out the news of my arrival. I took off my cap and wanted to yell with the crowd, not because I had gone around the world in seventy-two days, but because I was home again.

XVIII

The Record

I started from Hoboken, on my trip, around the world, November 14, 1889. I finished it in Jersey, January 25, 1890. The itinerary of my trip, published the morning I started, and the itinerary as I found it, were as follows:

Nov. 14–Leave New York by Augusta Victoria, 9.30 A.M.	Nov. 14–Left New York via Augusta Victoria.
" 21–Due Southampton. London by rail in three hours.	
" 22–Leave Victoria Station, London, 8 P.M., on India Mail	" 22–2.30 A.M. Arrived Southhampton-London " 22–10.00 A.M. Left London, Charing Cross Station
" 23–Calais, Paris and Turin	" 23–1.30 A.M. Left Calais
" 24–Brindisi at 10.14 P.M.	
" 25–Leave Brindisi, steamship Cathay, 9 A.M.	" 25–1.30 A.M. Arrived Brindisi. 3.00 A.M. Left Brindisi, steamship Victoria
" 27–Ismallia.	" 27–3.30 P.M. Arrived Port Said.
	" 28–11.00 A.M. Arrived Ismallia, 9.00 P.M. Suez.
Dec. 3–Aden.	Dec. 3–11.00 Arrived Aden.
" 10–Colombo (Ceylon).	" 8–11.00 A.M. Arrived Colombo (Ceylon).
" 16–Penang.	" 16–7.00 A.M. Arrived Penang.
" 18–Singapore.	" 18–5.00 A.M. Arrived Singapore.
" 25–Hong Kong.	" 25–7.00 A.M. Arrived Hong Kong.

" 28–Leave Hong Kong for Yokohama, Japan.	" 28–2.30 P.M. Left Hong Kong for Yokohama.
Jan. 7–Leave Yokohama, via Pacific Mail Steamship.	Jan. 7–10.55 A.M. Left Yokohama via Occidental and Oriental Steamship.
" 22–Due San Francisco.	" 21–8.00 A.M. Arrived San Francisco
	" 23–7.05 A.M. Arrived Chicago.
" 27–Due New York.	" 25–3.51 P.M. Arrived New York.
Nov. 14 to Jan. 27–seventy-five days.	Nov. 14 to Jan. 25–Seventy-two days.

	Miles	Hours Traveling	Hours Delayed
Hoboken to Southampton	3,041	184 50	50
To London	90	2 15	14 25 *
" Brindisi	1,450	53 30	1 30
" Port Said	930	62 30	3 30
" Aden	1,394	110	6
" Colombo	2,093	138	98 05
" Penang	1,278	89 55	7
" Singapore	381	39	11
" Hong Kong	1,437	111	127 20
" Yokohama	1,597	131 40	104 55
" San Francisco	4,525	333 05	
" Chicago	2,573	71 05	2 55
" Jersey City	951	29 51	
	21,740	1356 41	377 30

Total time occupied in tour, 1,734 hours and 11 minutes, being 72 days, 6 hours and 11 minutes.

Average rate of speed per hour, exclusive of stops, 22.47 miles.

Average rate of speed, including stops, 28.71 miles per hour.

The names of the steamers and the different routes by which I traveled were the "Augusta Victoria" of the Hamburg American Steamship Line, the London and South Western Railway, the South Eastern Railway, the India Mail, the "Victoria" and the "Oriental" of the Peninsular and Oriental Steamship Line, the "Oceanic," of the Occidental and Oriental Steamship Line, the Southern Pacific Railway, the Atlantic and Pacific Railway, the Atchison, Topeka and Sante Fé Railway and the Pennsylvania Railway.

I spent 56 days 12 hours and 41 minutes in actual travel and lost by delay 15 days 17 hours and 30 minutes.

The second table shows the miles traveled, hours spent in traveling and hours delayed. The "hours delayed" marked by a star shows the time spent in diverging from my original line of travel to visit M. and Mme. Jules Verne at Amiens. I traveled 179-½ miles out of my way to visit the great novelist which is not considered in my number of miles traveled, nor do I count the miles traveled at the ports where I was detained, which taken together would not fall short of 1,500 miles.

Up to date, my trip is the fastest on record between San Francisco and Chicago. One run was 250 miles in 250 minutes, and that, counting the minutes lost stopping at a half dozen different towns. Another run was 59 miles in 50 minutes. Between Topeka and Kansas City we ran 13 miles in 11 minutes. Later we ran a mile in 53 seconds, and again 26 miles in 23 minutes. We made 2,566 miles in 69 hours, which is the fastest time, I am informed, that has been made for this distance. Although the Sante Fe route is over 500 miles longer than the Union Pacific, we beat the time of the fastest mail to Chicago by ten hours. If we had had the same distance to travel we would have beaten it twenty-four hours. The Santa Fé had only one day to prepare for my trip, and yet everything was perfect. They tell me when the Palmer-Jarrett "Across the Continent" trip was made they had been preparing for it for six months in advance, and when the start was made a flagman was posted at every switch and crossing between New York and San Francisco, and yet without any preparations my train traveled 500 miles farther and beat their time by 24 hours.

It is not possible to quote my fares and expenses as a criterion for prospective tourists, as I was traveling for a newspaper, and what it cost is their secret. Not counting the extra train, if first-class tickets had been bought from New York to New York it would only have cost $805. By using economy, outside expenses should not exceed $300.

On my tour I traversed the following waters: North River, New York Bay, Atlantic Ocean, English Channel, Adriatic Sea, Ionian Sea, Mediterranean Sea, Suez Canal, Gulf of Suez, Red Sea, Straits of Bab el Mandeb, Gulf of Aden, Arabian Sea, Indian Ocean, Straits of Malacca, China Sea, Pacific Ocean, San Francisco Bay.

I visited or passed through the following countries: England, France, Italy, Egypt, Japan, the United States, and the following British possessions: Aden, Arabia; Colombo, Isle of Ceylon; Penang, Prince of Wales Island; Singapore, Malay Peninsula; and the Island of Hong Kong.

L'ENVOI

To so many people this wide world over am I indebted for kindnesses that I cannot, in a little book like this, thank them all individually. They form a chain around the earth. To each and all of you, men, women and children, in my land and in the lands I visited, I am most truly grateful. Every kind act and thought, if but an unuttered wish, a cheer, a tiny flower, is imbedded in my memory as one of the pleasant things of my novel tour.

From you and from all those who read the chronicle of my trip I beg indulgence. These pages have been written in the spare moments snatched from the exactions of a busy life.

A Note About the Author

Nellie Bly (1864-1922) was an American investigative journalist. Born Elizabeth Jane Cochran in a suburb of Pittsburgh, Pennsylvania, she was raised in a family of Irish immigrants. In 1879, she attended Indiana Normal School for a year before returning to Pittsburgh, where she began writing anonymously for the Pittsburgh Dispatch. Impressed by her work, the newspaper's editor offered her a full-time job. Writing under the pseudonym of Nellie Bly, she produced a series of groundbreaking investigative pieces on women factory workers before traveling to Mexico as a foreign correspondent, which led her to report on the arrest of a prominent Mexican journalist and dissident. Returning to America under threat of arrest, she soon left the Pittsburgh Dispatch to undertake a dangerous investigative assignment for Joseph Pulitzer's New York World on the Women's Lunatic Asylum on Blackwell's Island. After feigning a bout of psychosis in order to get admitted, she spent ten days at the asylum witnessing widespread abuse and neglect. Her two-part series in the New York World later became the book Ten Days in a Mad-House (1887), earning Bly her reputation as a pioneering reporter and leading to widespread reform. The following year, Bly took an assignment aimed at recreating the journey described in Jules Verne's Around the World in Eighty Days (1873). Boarding a steamer in Hoboken, she began a seventy-two day trip around the globe, setting off a popular trend that would be emulated by countless adventurers over the next several decades. After publishing her book on the journey, Around the World in Seventy-Two Days (1890), Bly married manufacturer Robert Seaman, whose death in 1904 left Bly in charge of the Iron Clad Manufacturing Co. Despite Bly's best efforts as a manager and inventor, her tenure ultimately resulted in the company's bankruptcy. In the final years of her life, she continued working as a reporter covering World War I and the women's suffrage movement, cementing her legacy as a groundbreaking and ambitious figure in American journalism.

A Note from the Publisher

Discover more of your favorite classics with Bookfinity™.

- Track your reading with custom book lists.
- Get great book recommendations for your personalized Reader Type.
- Add reviews for your favorite books.
- AND MUCH MORE!

Visit **bookfinity.com** and take the fun Reader Type quiz to get started.

Enjoy our classic and modern companion pairings!

Printed in the USA
CPSIA information can be obtained
at www.ICGtesting.com
JSHW082348140824
68134JS00020B/1955

9 781513 280066